Praise fo.
Body of Work

"Why does the album endure in the streaming age? Keith Jopling's neat treatise on the album as an artistic format provides the answer, taking in the history of the album, the technological changes of the music industry, the artistic drive that the LP format fulfils, and some personal reflections along the way. A clear-headed summation of the album's evergreen appeal."

Will Hodgkinson, Chief Rock and Pop Critic, *The Times*

"Keith Jopling, at once advocate and analyst, has written an affectionate and insightful account of the album's survival in a hostile age of streaming and algorithms."

Ludo Hunter-Tilney, Arts and Pop Critic, *FT*

"The internet can scale just about anything, but it can't scale the intimacy of exploring an artist's body of work, and the album's resilience is captured in this remarkable book."

Will Page, author of *Tarzan Economics*

"This book made me fall in love with the art of the album again, and I'm sure it will do the same for you. A must read for any true music fan."

Shain Shapiro, author of *This Must Be the Place*

"Is the album dead? It isn't and it is. We can therefore approach **Body of Work** *as a thought experiment: let's call it Schrödinger's catalogue. Jopling explores why the album is the historical anomaly that battled through multiple format shifts to (mostly) endure artistically, culturally, and economically.* **Body of Work** *is part eulogy for the album's past glories and part electioneering for the album's future relevance."*

Eamonn Forde, author of *The Final Days of EMI*

RIDING THE ROLLERCOASTER

Riding The Rollercoaster: how artists survive the music business to become the legends we love

Keith Jopling

Published by Repeater Books

An imprint of Watkins Media Ltd

Unit 11 Shepperton House

89-93 Shepperton Road

London

N1 3DF

United Kingdom

www.repeaterbooks.com

A Repeater Books paperback original 2026

1

Distributed in the United States by Random House, Inc., New York.

ISBN:9781917516358

Ebook ISBN: 9781917516365

Printed and bound by CPI Group (UK) Ltd, Croydon, CR0 4YY

This book is dedicated to the miracle of bands, and the force of nature that is the solo artist.
Artificial Intelligence will never replace you.

CONTENTS

Foreword: Them's the Brakes

If Olly Knights, singer and songwriter from Turin Brakes, had a time machine, he would whoosh back to 2007 and the recording sessions for the band's fourth album *Dark on Fire*. It was an album written for stadiums: ambitious, anthemic and powerful. The band had stepped up from an indie-folk outfit to a fully plugged-in band with top-flight producer Ethan Johns, and a large personnel of guest players that filled out their sound to something more expansive. Their previous two albums had both gone top ten in the UK, although the band had failed to follow up on 2003's top five hit *Pain Killer*. Instead, the catchy folk-pop single *Fishing for a Dream*, released in 2005, barely scraped into the top 40. For Turin Brakes, it was make-or-break time.

Although the band had originally signed to an independent label, Source Records, that company was bankrolled by Virgin Records, itself owned by the British major label EMI. In August 2007, Terra Firma, the private equity company run by Guy Hands, acquired EMI (both recorded music and publishing) for $6.6 billion. The deal has gone down in history as one of the most disastrous private equity deals in history, ending with a court battle between Terra Firma and its bankers on the deal, Citigroup, which subsequently took temporary control of EMI. While this last detail may seem tangential in the career of Turin Brakes, it isn't. It came close to ending their career. If bands had bosses (and thankfully, they do not) Turin Brakes had four of them at that point. None of them got on particularly well. And the higher up the chain, the lower the belief in Turin Brakes.

Back to that time machine. Olly Knights would have gone back to the start of the recording process for *Dark on Fire*, sat down with long-time bandmate (and lead guitarist) Gale Paridjanian, Ethan Johns and all involved, and would have told everyone to make the record even bigger – *more* epic, *more* ambitious, *more* cinematic – playing up the classic Americana sound the band was "messing with at the time". Had it been so, perhaps Virgin Records might have realised what they had on their hands – something as sweeping and emotional as any U2 album – all killer, no filler, as they say. Had the butterfly flapped its wings differently, Turin Brakes could have broken the USA and then gone huge worldwide.

Alas, that's not how it went. *Dark on Fire* was released in September 2007, amongst the first albums to be released by EMI under the new owners, Terra Firma. At that time, most people within the EMI empire were wondering how much longer they would be in a job. There was little appetite to persevere with a "difficult" record (i.e. one that wasn't an obvious hit to everyone in the building, including the bankers). *Dark on Fire* was a commercial flop, reaching number 36 on the UK album chart, and without a hit single. It wasn't long before the band was unceremoniously dropped. Without a label, they were then dropped by their management and subsequently their live booking agent. By the end of that year, Turin Brakes were left high and dry.

Almost two decades later, Turin Brakes are still in the game and have recently released album number 10, *Spacehopper*. The band have arrived in a good place, one of career enlightenment – permanently underrated by the music media but ever-more appreciated by their hardcore fans. The long, hard climb back up the mountain began on a Friday evening in July 2012 with a gig at Hampton Pool, a suburban West London lido (capacity 300). The band even made an art film of guitarist Gale Paridjanian swimming a few lengths – might as well *bathe* in the obscurity, so to speak. It was a slow and steady resurrection from there, rebuilding their career step by step, working outside the mainstream of the music industry. The band could no longer rely on radio play or press coverage or get near the charts. Without a manager, they worked instead to a model of independence they called "the Robbie system", a tribute to the patient guidance and wisdom of their drummer (and de facto caretaker-manager) Rob Allum.

In effect, Turin Brakes got a head start on making their own way as an independent band, a model now not only preferred but sought after by their contemporaries and new bands alike. As of now, virtually *all* bands are independent. With a few rare exceptions, artists are not signed for long enough to regard themselves, or be regarded, as members of a label roster. One of the freedoms granted to truly independent artists and bands in the music business is creative control, granted by default when the music business realises it can no longer make any real money out of you. With their ninth album, 2023's *Wide-Eyed Nowhere*, the band hit another creative high and maintained that standard with 2025's *Spacehopper*.

The idea of a band over a quarter century into their career, well beyond their commercial peak yet making music at the top of their game, is truly inspiring. Yet the list of bands and artists joining this club is growing, from once-hyped bands like

Suede and Travis to those building slow-burn careers outside the mainstream, like Los Campesinos, Metric, Real Estate, Calexico, The Delines or Half Moon Run.

The *NME*'s assessment of Turin Brakes as a band starting out in 1999 was that they "inhabit a space which is entirely their own, fully formed and brutally emotive, there is nothing to compare them to." Some 25 years on, rock legend Robert Plant referred to the band as "The magnificent Turin Brakes". Plant played the band's song "Hope We Make It", from their sixth LP *Lost Property*. In the song, Knights sings:

The cards are stacked and out of whack
The wrong way down a one-way track
There's a wave of change that's rising
It starts inside a lonely soul
The pressure mounts and it takes its toll
There's a clear horizon line
Somewhere down the road
I hope we make it
Hope we make it through

Turin Brakes did indeed make it through. It may be a seemingly unremarkable story of a middling band's ability to grind it out, but many more artists and bands simply fall by the wayside, ending up on the scrapheap, chewed up and spat out by the ruthless music industry machine.

Compare Turin Brakes' career with that of their contemporaries The Thrills, a pop band formed in Dublin in 2001, also signed to Virgin Records. The band's debut album, *So Much for the City*, released in 2003 and produced by top-flight studio hand Tony Hoffer, was a hit, reaching number three in the UK and going platinum in both the UK and Ireland. The

Thrills' second album, *Let's Bottle Bohemia*, was a UK number one. Then, like Turin Brakes, the band aimed higher, looking for a bigger, more expansive sound. But they got bogged down. Third album *Teenager* took too long in the making, losing the band's all-important momentum. When it was eventually released in July 2007, a month before Terra Firma got its greasy hands on EMI, the album received positive reviews but had no clear single. It bombed, reaching only number 48 in the UK charts. Sometimes an early audience just isn't enough to carry you through. The band was inevitably dropped and entered an indefinite hiatus. Unlike Turin Brakes, they never came out of that slumber. The Thrills had, to all intents and purposes, imploded under the weight of ambition and expectation. Sadly, their story is much more typical than that of Turin Brakes. The remains of doomed indie bands, burnt out pop stars and faded singer-songwriters are scattered all around. But still, countless artists dare to dream of a successful career writing and performing songs until their ripe old age. Only a few make it, and most that do settle for cult status; strictly fans only, with the 'limelight' of the mainstream long faded, reduced to simply a fleeting moment of what we once referred to as fame.

PART 1
WELCOME TO THE STATIONS OF THE CROSS

The long-term success of music artists is something that has fascinated me for as long as I've worked in the music industry, some 25 years now. What sustains a career in a business notorious for a dangerously high rate of failure? How do bands and solo artists navigate the machinations of a business in which nothing is certain, other than that no one really has your back? It is the artist's work – made in a vacuum of creativity – that provides the fuel that powers the entire music business: record labels, publishers, streaming platforms, the touring industry, music festivals, the vinyl business, industry trade associations, royalty collecting societies, music media, press and public relations – the livelihoods of everyone involved. None of it could exist without the music and the people who make it. The fruits of their labour provide for the careers of well over a million people that work directly in the music industry and plenty more on the periphery. The phenomenal success of streaming platforms like Spotify has fuelled a more exploitative form of capitalism in the music business in which large corporations and investors can make greater profits than ever, but the artists continue to work without a safety net in a global gig economy. No pun intended.

It is pretty shocking how artists are treated. They might be wrapped in cotton wool and fawned over when they are 'baby artists' and while things are on the up and up, but consistent sound advice is often thin on the ground. Who really has their career interests (and their personal wellbeing) at heart over the long term? You might assume it is the manager, and to some extent, it is. Managers do have a significant duty of care, which the best among them take very seriously, but they are businesspeople, not therapists. Managers are caught between a rock and a hard place, relying on music labels, publishers and technology platforms and doing their best to please all of them, which usually means pushing the artist to their limits. Meanwhile, looking after (usually multiple) musicians is more than a full-time job but often doesn't pay like one. Managers have their own career problems to worry about.

In 2021, I started *The Art of Longevity* podcast with the aim of interviewing established music artists with honest reflection and perspective. I explored with them what has brought long-term 'success', however they define it, and most define it in intrinsic, non-monetary terms – putting them directly at odds with almost everyone else on the 'business side' of things. How did they make it through the music industry mangle when many of their peers got chewed up and spat out? I wanted to find the answers first-hand from the artists themselves, not from managers, industry executives, journalists or other observers. I wanted to see if I could find common threads or themes that could explain why some artists and bands are more enduring. How much of it is down to talent, attitude, decision making, timing and luck? After some 80 episodes, this book is a summary of what I've discovered.

To steer the conversations through a narrative, *The Art of Longevity* podcast is based on a quote by Brett Anderson of British rock band Suede (once known in the USA as the London Suede). In the second half of his autobiography, *Afternoons with the Blinds Drawn*, Anderson wrote: "All successful artists have followed a similar career arc with the same points plotted grimly along the way like the Stations of the Cross: struggle, success, excess, disintegration, and if you're lucky – enlightenment."

A pithy (if rather gothic) summary of Suede's career but also a comment on the music industry, notorious for mobilising around artists on the way up but quickly backing away once the shine wears off and the going gets tough. The maxim "success has many fathers, failure is an orphan" perfectly describes how the music business works, with a posse of executives and tastemakers claiming some of the glory from artists in the ascendent while leaving the responsibility for failure squarely on the shoulders of those same artists. Record labels have always been ruthlessly happy to let artists fall by the wayside or 'drop' them, even those that were previously flavour of the month, or, in the record label vernacular, "a priority artist". A priority for who?

Often, after years of struggling to get noticed, artists are suddenly put on the pedestal of industry success – what the industry refers to as "breaking" an artist. Early success in the charts brings the glow of the limelight – video shoots, press features, radio interviews – drooling attention from all those around them. Since many artists have difficulty coping with fame and its aftermath, the word "breaking" might have a double meaning here. Whilst some might crave it, many artists do not want and cannot deal with the ridiculous, inauthenticity of fame, turning to drugs and/or alcohol to cope. Erratic behaviour and mental health issues inevitably arisé (the 'excess' phase of Brett Anderson's career curve).

Relationships, creative output and eventually, careers, are then damaged in the aftermath ('disintegration'). From there, how artists pick themselves up, dust themselves off and navigate a long-term career is akin to a marathon obstacle course. The achievement of success on their own terms – what Anderson calls 'enlightenment' – is ultimately the purpose of this book – i.e. how artists find a path to it.

In the book I focus on the themes and common threads that characterise artists and bands that have survived the ups and downs of the music industry rollercoaster to sustain their careers, reflecting on each and all of the 80 conversations, which act as case studies. Along the way, I reflect on a wider set of examples of well-known artists who have survived and thrived, often passing through Brett Anderson's 'Stations of the Cross' not just once but several times over.

I talk about artists, meaning bands and solo artists, interchangeably. But they are different. To my mind, a band is a miracle – multiple different people with differing, complementary talents who somehow find each other in the same time and place – and then go on and create songs, albums, perhaps legend. They are surrogate families that hold it together against the odds. The music they create is the result of "improbable synergies."[1] As for solo artists, they are forces of nature. Troubadours, de facto leaders, supreme talents with superhuman levels of bravery, self-belief and contradiction. With great talent comes great responsibility. The book refers to both and draws on many examples, and if I do use the word 'creator', then I really do mean it in the artistic sense.

The book is not a statistical analysis. I've tried that. There's no point approaching 'success' from a mathematical or

1 'Who Says Rock Is Dead?' Jon Pareles, *The New York Times*, January 2026.

scientific point of view when it comes to a musician's career in the music business. There are just too many random factors at work. And ultimately the word success has far too broad a meaning. However, for the artists featured, I do look at their chart histories and album reviews, consulting resources such as Album Of The Year and Metacritic (aggregated record reviews) and Ultimate Music Database (histories of UK and USA peak chart positions). If there is a persistent theme from these sources, it is that, ultimately, making consistently good music wins out over short-term commercial success, but the former doesn't usually come without the latter. There are a few exceptions of slow-burn ascendancy, and these are the lucky artists and bands who also managed to escape the trauma of fame. But more about that later.

I open the book with a few short chapters about how artists are, incredibly, still undervalued, even as they become more important to the ever-growing music industry in the encroaching age of artificial intelligence. The main section of the book is divided into two parts. The first part consists of five chapters on each of the major routes to longevity, with case studies of well-known artists and bands, along with a glimpse into the future for each of these major routes to success: hit songs, classic albums, record labels, cult status and branding. The second part consists of 21 themes of longevity based on insights and inspiration from the episodes of *The Art of Longevity* podcast. The book concludes with an outlook for how five current bands might grow to become legends and how the music industry can enable that to happen for more music creators in the future. If we want to keep on benefitting from being music fans, with our fandom growing alongside the career journeys of those artists we love, then we need to find a better way to nurture and look after new talent coming into the music industry today. That is the responsibility of the music business but us too, the listeners and fans.

Who is this book for?

For artists and musicians at all career stages, I hope that in reading this book, you will be inspired by those who have survived and thrived and as a result, manage your own career with more confidence, belief and resilience, especially during times of adversity. As Ed Robertson, the singer of Canadian music legends Barenaked Ladies told me: "The best part of the rollercoaster is the ride back down." Throughout our conversations about longevity, artists revealed themselves as musicians, singers, songwriters and creators, but also as leaders, pioneers, entrepreneurs and all round impressive human beings. They inspire and accompany the rest of us as we fumble our own way through life's ups and downs. Artists give of themselves; they relate to us. In doing so, they keep us company and provide us with a lifelong soundtrack. The work they do is powered by honesty and vulnerability, working through a capitalist system with very little empathy.

For those who work in the music business, directly with artists or indirectly, I hope the book will foster an even deeper appreciation and respect for how artists do what they do, despite all the hurdles and trapdoors put in front of them. Many in the industry share the dreams of artists but too easily forget that this should be the focus of each day they get to work with, and in service of, those artists. At the very least, this book might serve as an occasional reminder of that.

For music fans, if the book gives an insight into how the music industry works and deepens your admiration for these artists as a result, then all the better. And if it just encourages you to listen to the catalogues of those artists and bands mentioned or to go see them play live, I'm happier still. It's all too easy these days, when we are bombarded with content, to forget who our favourite bands are, and why we loved them in the first place.

I am deeply grateful to every artist who joined me as a guest on the podcast and spoke so frankly and with wisdom and gratitude. This book would not be possible without them and their incredible work.

Artists vs. the Music Business

In 2010, Radiohead singer Thom Yorke was quoted in a student textbook, predicting that the music business would collapse within "a matter of months". While the industry was undoubtedly going through a bumpy patch then, it was also at that time a Swedish start-up was beginning to cause a buzz in the business. Behind closed doors, music company executives were furtively whispering the word "growth" to each other after a decade of disruption and decay caused by Napster and internet piracy. To be fair to Thom Yorke, the immediate picture, as the music business transitioned from the strange years of iTunes downloads into the end game of streaming, did not look great. Yorke later famously declared Spotify not to be the industry's destiny but instead "the last desperate fart of a dying corpse".

Although Yorke probably doesn't enjoy reflecting on those words these days, it's not because he turned out to be wrong, but because it represented his sheer frustration with the business of music. He simply spoke to the belief of most artists, who would have been happy to see the back of the music business as it was – hoping that a better alternative might crop up in its place. But nothing did. Instead, Spotify pumped oxygen into the music business without disrupting the ecosystem of how the industry operates. Indeed, in the booming streaming era, music has become even more of a commodity. As streaming subscriptions have replaced CDs and downloads, the music industry keeps on getting bigger, and the much-maligned major labels have become even more powerful.

The fact that music companies and the artists contracted to do business with them survived the music industry downturn in the aftermath of Napster is a minor miracle. But what emerged in the streaming era is a more complex system in which the traditional music industry became enslaved to the major tech platforms, at whatever price point *they* decided could work for music – not as a product to buy occasionally but as a daily utility to be consumed. As a result, the artist – the source of the industry's value – ended up with less job security and take-home pay than just about everyone else in the music business.

I won't attempt to fix these problems within the pages of this book but simply frame how artists – not always respected for their business savvy – cope with this situation. If Thom Yorke was frustrated with the music business when he made his remarks in 2010, some 15 years on, many artists are even more frustrated now. Along with the tech and streaming platforms commodifying their works, they now have social media to contend with, with its insatiable appetite for 'content'. Artists must now also be content creators; videographers and influencers, along with their day jobs of writing, recording and performing songs. It means that releasing a song comes with a hefty amount of additional baggage: video clips, social media posts, remixed or sped-up versions of songs, or just related *sounds*. It's an impossible list of demands, many of them distractions from making actual songs. Meanwhile, despite all this extra work, artists are now finding that it is harder than ever to make a living in a business that generates more than $100 billion each year.[2] The music industry has seen a return to growth in the streaming era, with investment pouring into music and music tech, launching hundreds of new start-ups, all of it fuelled by the increase in songs being released by music artists at all career stages.

But, if the artist is the goose that lays the music industry's golden eggs, then who is looking after the goose? The music business appears to have no qualms about biting the hand that feeds. Artists frequently vent about their frustrations of creating art within a capitalist ecosystem – one increasingly dominated and dictated by global tech firms. Technology has enabled capitalism on a whole new level for the corporations operating in the music industry but that largely excludes the artist. No wonder global superstars like Sting, Bob Dylan and Bruce Springsteen decided to cash in their chips and sell off their songwriter copyrights to global investment funds and music majors while music is trading at an all-time high.

I'm not saying that on a day-to-day level, artists and their various industry representatives don't get on. Artists put their faith in their teams, and for the most part, managers, A&R reps, label marketers are all doing their best and pulling the same direction. The problem is that the system in which they are working is heavily rigged. Only in rap and hip-hop does music seem to blend well with business, and only then because in that world, artists have embraced capitalism, as described in books like *The Hip-Hop MBA* by Nels Abbey and *The Big Payback* by Dan Charnas. It doesn't always set a blueprint worth following, however, and artists in other music genres

2 Analysis by the consultancy firm OC&C suggests $106 billion revenues from all 'core music categories' in 2024

have yet to embrace the business side of music in the same way. In most cases, it seems like artists really have no appetite for the business side of things – not in the current set up. As Jim James, singer and songwriter of the band My Morning Jacket described the music business on *The Art of Longevity*:

> It's a really strange environment. For our first four or five records, people were still buying CDs which was a source of income for the band along with touring. Then iTunes came in and it was kind of confusing, but once streaming came in, you get *nothing* for your music. It's really fascinating that nobody quite understands why it is this way, and when anybody tries to do anything about it, it seems to have no effect. It is a puzzle, and we're all kinda trapped in this thing.

The truth is that most artists just do not like the record business and see it very much as a Faustian pact. It really shouldn't be that way, but will it ever change? I wonder sometimes how artists feel when walking into the concrete & glass temples of major label offices. They may feel the first buzz of success, until they get the uncomfortable idea that somewhere along the line, they are paying for the lavish surroundings and salaries of the people occupying that space. Artists are intrigued by the business, and yet perhaps feel they don't fully grasp it, and so must place their trust in those that do. And yet, they invariably know more about it than they realise. Meanwhile, across the other side of the table, music executives hold the artists in some reverence. Many execs are either failed artists or could only dream of a creative career themselves. Or, like the rest of us, they are just fans. It's a chalk and cheese situation that doesn't always make for an honest working relationship. A really strange environment indeed.

At the 2025 annual general meeting of the UK artist's lobbying and networking organisation, the Featured Artist's Coalition (FAC), a discussion panel of four artists were unanimous that their new year's resolution for the music business in 2026 would be for artists to 'get paid'. The panel was in no doubt about two facts; first, being a professional musician (or attempting to become one) is enormously hard work. It's non-stop. Secondly, that the work is not financially rewarding. Of course, music is a passion, besides who said that 'successful' musicians should automatically become rich and famous? The digital revolution ushered in the age of the 'middle class musician', whereby even a well-known and established professional artist is one that might earn the equivalent of a half-decent salary rather than one who ends up living in a mansion in London, a house in the Hollywood Hills or a castle in Scotland. It seems that the streaming era however, has brought about the age of the *working* class musician, one who often must look to earn a living either through additional part-time jobs on top of their artistic career, or via as many ancillary income streams as possible – be that selling merchandise, teaching, or being constantly busy producing and writing music for others.

But separately from poor remuneration, the industry doesn't make it easy for artists to *not* work. There is a multitude of never-ending tasks that demand you never to get a decent break, let alone the luxury of actual time off. In one of many gaffs when talking about artists, Spotify's ex-CEO Daniel Ek notoriously suggested to artists that: "you can't record music once every three to four years and think that's going to be enough", instead advising artists to produce content more frequently to succeed in the modern streaming era. Much of the extra work isn't what artists really want to be doing. On the FAC panel, the singer-songwriter Orla Gartland – a success on streaming platforms by any measure (with over 500 million monthly listeners) – described the working cycle of a musician as "the horseshoe of pain". At one end, writing and recording music is truly privileged and satisfying work. At the other end, performing that music to your fans is even better, very much living the dream. But the problem is all the stuff in-between – content creation, promo, networking, record label meetings, maintaining a constant presence across social media platforms.

For artists, working within the rules of the game, i.e. promoting yourself, is a necessity that comes with the territory – an occupational hazard. But artists really *do* want an audience, so why the reticence to do 'promo'? Why deny the fact that once you have created your art, if you want anyone to hear it, then you have got to sell it? Exposure is part of the artist's job description. As the post-genre, classically trained pianist and singer-songwriter Chilly 'Gonzo' Gonzales told me:

> If you want to be an artist and *not* live from it, by all means make art for yourself. But if you want to *live* from it, then throw your hat in the ring. It's ridiculous to force the myth of artistic purity. If you decide to put music out and find a fanbase, then own it.

Before a label can decide to invest in the sums required to break a star – easily into the millions of dollars at the higher end – they need to know if the artist, the musician, is willing to do whatever it takes to be just that – a star. Of course, many don't know until they try whether they can cope with the demands and the excesses of fame, especially in today's 24-7 global fishbowl, where stalker fans and social media influencers have replaced music snob journalists and A&R people as the primary providers of 'feedback'.

Mostly, artists *are* still game. Yet the industry can be a crude, blunt instrument. Marketers want to put you in a box, literally package your music into a digestible, sellable style or genre. Yet so many artists reject the idea of being labelled, finding it irritating or even insulting. 'Folk' duo The Lumineers laugh at being badged folk. 'Shoegaze' band Ride never liked the term used to describe their sound. 'Post Rock' band Mogwai are averse to that term. The way music is evolving, the most accomplished artists are bending and blending genres, and would prefer not to be put in a box. But tough. Not everybody can be Bob Dylan and do whatever they like.

For artists, the label's job is to sell your music – but also to sell *you*. As such, there is little room for nuance. The label wants to put you in a clear lane: a defined music genre, a clear brand identity, a target audience, and yet, also, potential broad appeal. Meanwhile, streaming services want to tag your music and reduce it to data for the algorithms. As for the music press (what's left of it), journalists will give you a badge to carry around your neck for decades. How many times has Bon Iver been described as a "reclusive who makes music in a log cabin"? Too many times. No wonder this environment can feel treacherous. In a system you might assume is there to help you, there are forces at work *against* you. It shouldn't be that way.

The music industry marks success by chart position, streaming counts, awards and social media statistics. To music industry executives, success means *commercial* success. Yet artists are rarely nourished by numbers. They receive validation through hearing stories of how fans connect with their music. They enjoy seeing the reactions of the crowd at shows. They are delighted when their quieter songs end up ranking high on streaming services alongside their 'hits'. What motivates the business side and artistic side of the business are poles apart.

When it comes to achieving success, it is the artist who should hold their business partners to account, not the other way around. The music you create as the artist *is the commerce*. I would suggest to all artists, lean into that. Be your own CEO, Creative Director or Commercial Director – be your own Board! Nobody else is going to do that on your behalf, not even your manager. Remember that the industry is built on the foundations of your work. *Your* brand is bigger than any other in the business. Don't let anyone tell you otherwise. For any artist entering the arena, it's worthwhile bearing in mind that whatever happens to you doesn't reflect the real you, and that keeping hold of what makes you real is an essential way to ride the music industry rollercoaster.

In other words, hold on tight to your dreams.

Old Songs vs. New Songs

Music is unique from other entertainment in that it ages well. We don't spend time watching footage of old sports games, and watching old movies is strictly for film buffs, but music is different. People discover music that is new to them on streaming every day, and don't really care when that music came out. 'Catalogue music' (officially defined as 18 months past first release date) makes up some three quarters of music streamed. The good news for artists of longevity is that older music can find new, replenished audiences. This has been a boon to the careers of older artists, an opportunity for them to tour, return to the festival circuit and make new records.

On the flip side, for *new* artists making *new* music, it's a daunting prospect that every new song competes not just with other new songs, but with all the world's music. This means that new artists have a drastically reduced chance of making the kind of cultural impact with their music that older artists once did. Having a hit is hard. Making an album of any lasting impact is even harder. Making enough money to carry on trying is almost impossible. No wonder older artists express gratitude for launching their careers before the flood of streaming and social media. And no wonder newer artists fret over numbers and hang onto every possible fleeting moment of success. In the book *The Endless Refrain*, veteran music journalist David Rowell tries to answer the question "Do we even *want* new music anymore?" It's a provocation of course. Rowell realises that we do, but still, maybe music is just not quite as good as it used to be? Many songs that work their way up the global streaming charts today do seem a little… disposable. YouTuber and music producer Rick Beato regularly works his way through a musical analysis of the Spotify Top 50 in his series *The Death of Memorable Songs*. You can guess his conclusions. Stats guru Daniel Parris analysed the staying power of current songs on his *Stat Significant* blog, concluding: "Gone are the days when a song's popularity built slowly through word-of-mouth and radio airplay, now replaced by instant surges of premeditated virality."

However, reviewing Spotify Top 50 data from number-crunching platform Chart Metric, Parris also found that enough songs squeezed through the gaps to find lasting success: "While nearly half of Spotify Top 50 tracks vanish after just one week on the charts, a surprising 20% of trending tunes endure for 90 days or more; evidence that durable hits like "Espresso" [Sabrina Carpenter] and "Hot to Go!" [Chapell Roan] can persist within the zeitgeist for extended periods of time".

Some new songs still undoubtedly have staying power. Try telling a 20-year-old Lana Del Rey fan they won't be singing "Summertime Sadness" at their 40th birthday party. Or that Sam Fender fans won't belt out "Seventeen Going Under" when they are 37 or over. New songs connect with their fans in the same way songs always did. The songs we hear in our formative years are the ones that stay with us for life. That still applies to young people.

Why Longevity Matters

A career in music might be a divine calling for artists but it is not the most solid way to make a living, especially in today's hyper-competitive and multi-fragmented music market. It's harder to succeed as a new artist now, when content is saturated and your music must cut through the clutter, rise above everything else, not just once but repeatedly. Artists that achieve a modicum of early success – a hit song or a well-received album – must somehow find the creativity and resources to do it all over again. And then *again*. Maintaining a career in music means working through entrenched album cycles, with each, depending on the artist's career stage and work rate, taking several years. Since streaming went mainstream, touring has become the principal way to make real money for artists (although that too is increasingly, and worryingly, difficult). To tour, you will need a new album. That requires writing, rehearsing and recording at least ten songs (but in practice many more than that) and then spending many months promoting your new project. Artists spend a year or two of their life on the creation of a new album, something Daniel Ek failed to grasp.

Breaking this cycle can often be the first real sign of career longevity. Once artists have enough quality material in their catalogue, they can instead tour to support key album anniversaries, re-release their classic albums or archive material, or work on side projects. Some can even take precious time off. But to get there involves many years, a decade or more, working within the album-cycle system. Over the years, as artists work their way through several album cycles, they must stay relevant as tastes change, music media switches focus to newer bands, fanbases get older and become interested in things other than music. Navigating the territory of how to develop a musical style without alienating early fans or isolating yourself from gatekeepers is not a cakewalk.

In *Exit Stage Left: The Curious Afterlife of Pop Stars*, author Nick Duerden colourfully explores what happens to those artists who, having once been – however briefly – placed on the pedestal of fame, struggle to cope with the idea of reduced attention for the remainder of their compromised careers:

> They have had their time in the sun, their three ironclad years, and they may have been forcefully shuffled to the margins by tastemakers wielding figurative brooms, but they don't really go away; they don't disappear and stop doing what they've always done. *Of course* they don't – they're *artists*, that breed of humans who were never cut out for the traditional nine-to-five, for the daily commute, for cookie-cutter conventionality. So even after they've reluctantly parted ways with the zeitgeist, the songs keep coming, they keep plugging away.[3]

I want to explore more deeply not just *why* the songs keep coming and artists keep plugging away, but *how* they do it, what choices they make and how they come to see continuity and longevity as success itself. The idea of survival, with an element of thriving beyond the shallow affirmation of music industry accolades and success metrics. Duerden's book is

---

3 *Exit Stage Left*, Nick Duerden. Headline, p.14.

something of a curiosity, as it covers a number of obscure artists who have fallen by the wayside, such as Ed Tudor-Pole (a UK chart one-hit wonder from 1981, as Tenpole Tudor). Yet the book also covers enduringly successful artists, including folk legend Shirley Collins and legendary singer-songwriter Suzanne Vega. Duerden includes chapters on David Gray, Robbie Williams and Rufus Wainwright and it could be argued that all of them have had continued success even though they certainly benefited from some time in the limelight, Duerdin's "three ironclad years".

David Gray certainly experienced a form of 'post-fame syndrome'. And yet he appears to have found a contentment – a resolution of his early struggle to break through and his subsequent experience with fame. Gray had been on the Manchester 'new folk' circuit for a decade before his self-recorded album *White Ladder* became a huge hit. He then enjoyed a second decade as a high profile 'priority artist', before settling into a more modest status. As for longevity, Gray is comfortably across the Rubicon, some 30 years into and moving towards the next phase of his career. On a creative and productive songwriting streak and with a sold-out world tour in 2025, he seems more motivated than at any time in his career as a sometimes pugilistic singer-songwriter: "I've got clear space to move on. When you've already passed 'Go', there is a whole labyrinth of decisions to make and paths you can take."

With *Exit Stage Left*, Duerden was looking to explore and explain post-fame adjustment, a sort of celebrity version of post-traumatic stress disorder. How musicians could carry on after their brief time in the spotlight. With *The Art of Longevity*, my assumption is that artists are self-aware enough to know that their time in the sun is fleeting and that the reality of a career is what happens after the first flushes of fame. Somehow, they must disassociate career continuity from the music industry's tendency to gaslight its talent base. As Elton John puts it, when discussing the relative commercial failure of his later albums in *Me:*

> I've had my moment selling zillions of records, and it was fabulous, but the second it began, I realised it wouldn't last forever. If you believe it will, you can end up in terrible trouble. I honestly think that's what tipped Michael Jackson over the edge: he was convinced he could make an album bigger than *Thriller* and was crushed every time it didn't happen.[4]

When it comes to lasting the distance, nobody knows it like Sir Elton John.

An artist's real career is their time after the limelight; the renaissance or 'enlightenment', as Brett Anderson puts it. Their real career is the undistorted world of loyal fans, viable touring, modest record sales and half-decent reviews. And hopefully, enough money to keep going. Post-limelight creative successes may not include chart hits but can still bring a meaningful mid-career boost. On the other hand, trying to hang on to fame, money or cultural relevance is no way to build a lasting and successful career. Be grateful for it but be prepared to let fame go. Robbie Williams, very much a momentum pop star and self-confessed 'professional attention seeker', wisely said in an interview with *The Guardian*: "That's

4 *Me*, Elton John. Macmillan, p. 296.

another one of those confusing things about our job – that we constantly revisit the past to propel our careers forward."[5]

Some time ago the music production guru Rick Beato uploaded a video to his YouTube channel in which he asked, "Why do we stop listening to our favourite artists?" In an engaging clip, Beato compares an old song with a new song by two of his old favourites, Depeche Mode and Tori Amos, admitting that for both he is something of a lapsed listener despite remaining a fan. Beato seems genuinely blown away by how much he likes their latest releases and vows to spend more time listening to the new albums by both artists. But the reactions to this video are revealing in how almost everyone has the same habit of failing to keep up with new material from their old favourite bands. Life moves on. Priorities change. One responder to Rick's video names this "lapsed fan syndrome". On top of all the challenges for artists that break through and achieve success in the music business, contending with lapsed fan syndrome feels like the hardest. *The Guardian*'s chief music critic Alexis Petridis wrote (in a review for rock band Paramore's 2023 album *This Is Why*): "Growing up with your fans is not an easy thing to do: artists frequently end up trapped at the point in their careers where they had their biggest success, offering a welcome burst of nostalgia for which fans endure a few new songs as payment."

Holding onto fans is hard. You just can't take all of them with you as your career progresses. Fortunately, the Internet comes in handy in this regard. TikTok has become a music industry phenomenon due to its ability to introduce older classic songs to younger audiences, most famously boosting

5 "'Fame is a drug like LSD': Robbie Williams on success, sexuality and his simian movie alter ego," Micheal Cragg, *The Guardian*. Friday 13 December, 2024.

the late career of Fleetwood Mac thanks to a video of a middle-aged man on a skateboard holding onto the back of a truck and lip-synching to their 1977 track "Dreams". Meanwhile, YouTube's influence on music continues to grow. YouTube's algorithm serves up trending and relevant content irrespective of its age, perhaps even favouring older stuff with cultural authority. As a result, music discovery today is untethered from listener demographics, something that has liberated music in unexpected ways. It's a remarkable experience to go to a gig now for almost any established band or artist. Audiences consist of people of all ages and those singing the loudest often weren't born when the song's lyrics were written. Old music is no longer contained within 'golden oldie' radio formats. That is good news for artists who intend to stick around.

Take British pop band Duran Duran, one of the best examples of a band that has ridden the music industry rollercoaster several times over. Duran Duran had a stratospheric rise like no other band, elevated to massive global success in the 80s. During their golden period, anything other than a number one single would have been considered a disappointment. The 1984 tour documentary *Sing Blue Silver,* filmed at the height of their fame, follows the band around Canada and the United States as they tour (third album) *Seven and the Ragged Tiger*. It paints a vivid and glossy picture of young fame: photo shoots, radio interviews, backstage parties, celebrity meet and greets, even a Beatles-esque press conference. It also captures the hard graft of touring and performing, backstage antics, tour bus boredom and of course fanatical, adulating fans – at that time mostly teenage girls. The band members seemingly take everything in their stride, as famous musicians with record company contracts were expected to do in the 80s. While much has changed since then, many artists will recognise that this is still a prevailing characteristic of the music business – the artist is expected to do everything required to succeed – gruelling tours, endless PR engagements, and, in the modern age, limitless social media content creation. Exhaustion is part of the deal.

Inevitably, for Duran Duran, that level of success couldn't be sustained. The band had a more challenging 90s and then a whole decade of being virtually forgotten about – something they struggled with psychologically (and financially). By 1998, the once "fab five" (each with their own adoring fanbase, because back then everyone knew members of bands by name) was reduced to a core of just two: Simon Le Bon and Nick Rhodes, making somewhat bizarre records (*Medazzaland* and *Pop Trash* might be categorised as peculiarities in the Duran catalogue) and touring relatively small venues. During media and press appearances, for which Le Bon and Rhodes continued to dutifully turn up in the hope of promoting new material, questions would inevitably be about the height of their fame in the 80s, and the two would answer these tiresome questions through gritted teeth. They sucked it up.

When the original line-up reformed as a five-piece in 2004, it gave Duran Duran a spark from which to reignite their career. The band's new management helped build them back up, brick by brick, this time as an independent band: new record and touring deals, but most critically, a focus on the core fanbase through a new website, fan club and active social media presence. Each member of the band (except for guitarist Andy Taylor who soon departed again after the reformation) was again willing to do whatever it took – only differently to the first time around in the 80s. This time, they worked hard but smart. Older and wiser, Simon Le Bon and his famous bandmates kept their egos in check and put their relationships to the fore as equals in a band of some considerable influence and legend, all the while deliberately avoiding the 'nostalgia circuit' that drew in many of their 80s counterparts. Now, Duran Duran headline major festivals and sell out impressively large touring venues. Their new records confidently sound fresh and yet knowingly reference their early work. They look set to enjoy a continued, yet more contented success, outside of the music mainstream they once craved so badly to stay within. It's an impressive longevity story.

When it comes to bands, there are many more examples and yet each one has a unique longevity story (it means that Brett Anderson's theory doesn't quite hold up, even if those Stations of the Cross are highly recognisable career stages). For solo artists, longevity is arguably even harder to achieve. While they do not have to contend with the tensions of relationships with other band members (though in reality, they often do have long-term collaborators), they are forging a path alone, de facto leaders of all who choose to accompany them. Elton John barely survived the 90s and 2000s. Almost every album he made was either a creative or commercial disappointment, sometimes both. Yet he began to thrive again in the streaming era by engaging with smart collaborators and producing clever remixes of his old hits. A blockbuster movie and those continued megatours obviously did no harm, but rather than become an old folks' entertainer, John has successfully reached an evergreen audience by embracing new channels and staying connected to emerging artists. John was the first artist to sign a record deal in perpetuity, for "the rest of his career" (with Universal Music in 2018). Just a decade earlier, with albums *The Captain and The Kid* (2006) and *The Union* (2010), he had heavily criticised his record company for not promoting his albums and outwardly called record label executives "idiots". Yet he and his music industry representatives clearly got over their differences to bring him back to the forefront of popular culture, the top of the singles charts, and even headlining Glastonbury (in 2023). It cannot have been easy. The entertainment analytics blog *Stat Significant* recently noted that Elton John has become *the* most longevous creator of chart hits. His 2022 hit *Cold Heart* reached number seven on the *Billboard* Hot 100 chart some 50 years after his first charting song, *Rocket Man*, peaked at number 20. I wonder which of those hits he has enjoyed most.

If you consider nothing unusual in the ongoing fortunes of the global superstar sitting at a piano, consider instead the career of the alternative indie artist sitting at a piano; take Australian singer-songwriter Nick Cave and his band The Bad Seeds, for example. Since the mid 80s, the band has enjoyed cult status with serious indie credibility and varying degrees of modest commercial success. Cave once declared in an interview that he had no idea why he sometimes seems to have plenty of money but then other times next to nothing at all, a comically effective description of the status of an indie band leader. Somehow, though, his status climbed very slowly to that of a solidly commercially successful star, without ever trying to become one. From having a number three UK chart album, *Push the Sky Away*, in 2013, Cave seems to have risen steadily to the point of being a household name. By 2024, Nick Cave & The Bad Seeds found themselves selling out arenas; one of a handful of indie bands with a hardcore loyal fanbase but a curious and growing wider audience. Never compromising on musical output, Cave and his long-term collaborators simply bided their time. There is always the chance that if you stay in the game long enough, you may reach newly elevated heights. Perhaps what the world needs right now is a modern-day preacher in a suit making sombre but strangely uplifting music, and with a sense of humour to boot. Sometimes it takes a long time to become suitably appreciated.

Speaking of Nick Cave, you may remember his surprise pairing with pop icon (and fellow Aussie) Kylie Minogue for the 1995 single "Where the Wild Roses Grow" (the Bad Seeds' only top 20 hit by the way). Minogue is a shining example of the pop career as a series of comebacks. From the unlikely beginnings as a TV soap star turned pop star by the machine-tooled hitmakers Stock, Aitken and Waterman in the late 80s, you would not have predicted that Kylie would still be in the UK top ten three decades on, but she was. Not only that, but look at how Minogue's profile as an artist has changed. The singer's 2023 hit "Padam Padam" was not just a return to form, but a good example of her ability to surprise and delight the music scene; the song was popular, credible – even *cool*. Her 2023 album, *Tension*, was her seventh number one UK album, following a triumphant 'legends' slot at Glastonbury 2019. And *that* was part of a comeback from undergoing breast cancer treatment. These days, Kylie Minogue is pop royalty: much admired and respected, not to mention influential. In 2025, she embarked on her biggest tour in over a decade. Often, one big song can bring you right back into popular culture, and it seems that, specifically, Minogue has a talent for unearthing those big songs.[6]

---

6 She did it again with the 2025 Christmas #1 in the UK chart, with the song "XMAS," making Kylie the first woman to top the singles chart in four different decades.

Will today's music superstars have longevity?

While we may have come out of the golden age of pop that produced Duran Duran, Elton John, Nick Cave & The Bad Seeds, and Kylie Minogue, it doesn't mean that we won't have future superstars and bands whose careers span decades and build impressive catalogues. Look at Taylor Swift. Setting new records for what it means to be a superstar, the unstoppable Swift was crowned Spotify's Global Top Artist in 2024 for the second year in a row, with 27 billion streams (she was second in 2025), in part due to the highest-grossing live show in history, *The Eras Tour.* Swift's self-titled debut came out in 2006, so she is approaching two decades as a top-flight commercial music artist. There is no better demonstration that legend status can still be achieved by a modern artist. However, Swift does precede the streaming age by a few years.

How about Spotify's Global Top Artist 2025, Bad Bunny? The Puerto Rican singer, rapper and producer (real name Benito Antonio Martínez Ocasio) was also 2022's most-streamed artist in the world on Spotify – for the third year in a row by that point. And even though Bad Bunny has only been releasing music commercially since 2018, with hit power like that, longevity seems assured, even though he may not become a global household name in the same way as Taylor Swift. Bad Bunny's 2025 album *DeBÍ TiRAR MáS FOToS* (I Should Have Taken More Photos), his sixth, may be hard to spell, but it receives a 90% critical rating on the aggregation site Album of the Year. The album leans more heavily into Puerto Rican tradition. By album number six, Bad Bunny has earned enough popular capital to make a creative lean to the left, something he might not have been able to pull off on a second or third outing. He has undoubtedly crossed the Rubicon to long-term commercial and creative success, and we can expect him to be around for decades. Streaming is an effective platform from which top-tier artists can achieve global dominance. The major record labels and top live music promoters now know that the current crop of global superstars are bigger than ever. Of the five most popular acts on Spotify in 2025, four of them also occupied the top five spots in 2022 and 2023. Three of them – Bad Bunny, Drake and The Weeknd – did the same in 2021 *and* 2020. Global dominance is important to longevity. The more prominent and sustained artists can become at the height of their success, the longer they get to stick around.

Streaming platforms now fulfil the role of cultural gatekeepers on a grand scale. They are music retailers, chart compilers, radio stations and media platforms rolled into one. Global superstars make up a tiny fraction of a growing community of professional musicians, however. They are one percent of the one percent, but what about the rest? This book features a bunch of distinguished and longevous artists, each of which has found a path to a long and successful career. Many of them had hits and achieved notable fame for a time, but others did not and still don't get much attention from those all-important industry gatekeepers. Yet they continue to thrive, many of them making the best work of their careers much later on. And this is why longevity matters. Artists who stick around continue to get better with experience. They may have creative (and commercial) peaks and troughs, but as they endure, and as we fans stick with them, we reap the benefits of their developing craft, accumulated wisdom, and everlasting creativity.

How do they do it?

PART 2
CROSSING THE RUBICON – FIVE ROUTES TO LONGEVITY

When I interviewed Brett Anderson on *The Art of Longevity* and asked him about his theory of a band's career, he was as contradictory as you might expect:

> I'm not sure longevity should necessarily be a goal. Longevity has come about because of my obsession with what I do. It's born from a recognition of my flaws – looking at what I've done in the past as a disappointment. As soon as you think you've done your best work, it's game over. The search for that point of perfection – the journey – is what it's about.

It's a sound philosophy in hindsight, although many artists starting out in music do think about longevity, however. They think about the possibilities that can come from a career: finding a loyal audience, making enough money to give up the day job, creating a body of work and leaving a legacy alongside their own inspirations. In other words, they dare to dream.

But how to achieve it? Throughout the conversations for *The Art of Longevity*, five pathways to long-term success emerged:

1. Have a 'hit' record.
2. Get dropped by your record label.
3. Make a 'classic' album.
4. Establish "quiet legend" aka cult status.
5. Build a brand aka become a band that is more than the sum of its parts.

There are many other factors, of course, and I explore these in the second part of this book – a digest of 20 themes for longevity. I've included the craft of live performance among these – a necessity for longevous artists but not a route to success by itself. If it was, Another Sky might not have split and the Milk Men would have topped the charts.

The above might be considered the 'big five', if you will. Achieve any combination of these and longevity is all but secured. The problem is that none of them are easy. The music industry keeps on changing and so do the rules of the game when playing the role of artist within that ecosystem. With the impending impact of artificial intelligence, the picture for actual, human artists will continue to change at an even faster pace than in the first century of recorded music. However, even in the age of AI music, I stand by the suggestions in this book – tried and tested as they are by so many amazing artists featured on *The Art of Longevity.*

By way of guidance, here are some considered thoughts on the five routes – past, present and future.

ROUTE 1 – HAVE A HIT RECORD

"The bigger the hit, the bigger the liability."
—Donny Osmond

Historically, a hit meant a high chart position, but these days, an impressive streaming count is what you need. The music business is run on hits, full stop. It is one big hit factory and unlikely to ever change. But streaming has changed the nature of hits. In fact, although a hit is more important now than ever, there is no longer any clear definition of what a hit really means.

A hit song is one that has notable, measurable success. Indeed, if you are an artist with any level of success by way of a popular song, streaming services like Spotify will remind you of that every day of your life, by pinning that popular song to the top of your profile page, with the number of streams right next to it. This is to remind you of how great you used to be and how your old stuff is so much better than anything you can create these days. See it as motivation.

There is no real agreed or designated threshold for what constitutes a streaming hit. The music industry associations, like the RIAA (Recording Industry Association of America) and BPI (British Phonographic Industry), do have certifications for singles based on "units sold" but nobody really understands what this means anymore, nor takes much notice. There are no units sold now, just tracks streamed for more than 30 seconds. What gets more attention is the Spotify Billions Club – the songs that have crossed the one billion streams threshold on the platform. Spotify has a rolling playlist and well over 1,000 songs have achieved a Spotify Billions Club plaque (yes, there is an actual plaque). One billion is an extremely large number, and the Billions Club remains out of reach for 99.99% of artists with music on Spotify. That's why the music writer Bobby Owsinski once summed up the question of how many streams it takes to make a hit with a simple: "more zeros than you think".

As a rule of thumb, if you have a song that reaches five million streams, you have something to shout about. Within a reasonable timeframe, accruing 10 million streams will give your label cause for excitement – the equivalent of hitting the top 20 in the 80s. At 50 million streams you have a bona fide hit from which you can make a reasonable amount of money – depending on the structure of your deal. More motivation. To be considered a major hit however, we're talking over 100 million streams – perhaps even the potential to join the Billions Club one day. Even David Bowie hasn't made it into the Billions Club (yet), unless you include "Under Pressure," his 1982 hit with Queen.

There have been dozens of books (and a few companies have been created) dedicated to the science of having a hit. Of course, the irony is, there is no science to it. One of my favourite quotes from *The Art of Longevity* podcast is from Steve Berlin, saxophonist and de facto band leader of L.A. Latin rock band Los Lobos, who said, "There is no formula for having a hit record; it's 60% luck, 30% talent and 10% timing." That throwaway line may be as valid as any formula created about scoring a hit record. No one can tell you *how* to do it, but plenty will tell you that you need to at some point – and the sooner the better. A hit is the on-ramp to the shortest possible route to 'success'. And record labels love "route one" (they are addicted to shortcuts).

Whether a band's career began with a hit song, or whether the hit came later, few artists would ever turn away from the idea of having a hit. Spoon, the indie band from Austin, Texas, achieved longevity without a hit song by making consistently good albums, revered by critics, as well as being a formidable live act. But as Britt Daniel told me, "It would be nice to have a hit". He's right, it wouldn't do the band any harm. Plenty of artists will, at some stage, make a song that *sounds like* a hit, but that's a long, long way from having one. Indeed, it might be the wrong approach to even try, since most songs that sound like hits, sadly never become one. Matthew Caws, lead singer and songwriter for the New York indie guitar band Nada Surf (who have never had a hit in 30 years but have produced ten very good albums) has banned the notion that during the recording process someone might suggest that a song "sounds like a hit", the very idea setting expectations that are bound to be a letdown. But hits can "break" an artist. They are the silver bullets by which the artist can impress industry gatekeepers and subsequently introduce them to a wider audience. For this reason, hits are at the top of every rising artist's priority list, certainly for those who have signed a record deal. A hit can take you a long way. The bigger the hit, the longer the halo effect. A hit can even provide you with a career that lasts for decades.

On the other hand, a hit can also be dangerous, in that it can too quickly come to define you. This is probably what Donny Osmond meant (see the above quote).

Here is another quote, this one from Maseo, member of hip-hop legends De La Soul, who told the UK *Guardian*: "On our second album, we learned the importance of controlling the narrative. I learned early on that a hit record can hurt your entire body of work if you let the industry control your narrative". Weirdly, the music business can occasionally work a hit record *against* you by insisting that you repeat the trick, which has a dangerous potential to backfire should it box you into a corner, creatively.

Some artists' biggest hit songs were released in a short, intense burst and these tracks were a springboard to a high-profile career. A prime example is KT Tunstall. Tunstall's 30-year journey as a professional musician is something of a classic model for longevity: a decade-long struggle to get signed, a stratospheric rise to the top as a priority artist on a major label, followed by a steady drop in record sales after her sophomore album *Drastic Fantastic* (2007). She then had years of wrestling between her own creative instincts and the commercial demands of the industry. As she stressed on *The Art of Longevity*: "There is a conflict of interest because you have made a piece of art that you love, and [the record label's] job is to sell it. You are put upon with all these comparative statistics – charts, awards, numbers – it's really unhelpful and not creative in any way".

What Tunstall describes is the ongoing conflict that arises in the music business – the awkward conflict between the creative goals of the artist and the commercial interests of their record label. This conflict drives so many contradictions in the music business. To judge success, the industry obsesses over numbers: sales and streaming stats, viral spikes and follower counts. But these metrics do not matter as much to artists. Artists see faces in the crowd and judge their own success on the strength of connection through live performance or perhaps gaining recognition amongst their peers. Priorities set by the music industry are not the same priorities for the artist. Artists don't want to make the same record twice, but labels (and maybe fans also) want them to repeat their success by sticking with the style that made them popular. Artists do not think in terms of genre, but the industry classifies them that way, with record stores and streaming playlists organised largely by genre definitions. These contradictions are confusing and frustrating for artists. Elbow's lead singer, enigmatic frontman Guy Garvey, describes this situation as the music industry mangle – since artists can feel like they are indeed being rinsed through a series of pain points. Success on their own terms is something to strive for once through "the mangle".

KT Tunstall understood that the record label's job is business, while her job is to make art. The Scottish singer-songwriter has released eight albums over two decades. Tunstall's three biggest hits came from her debut album *Eye to the Telescope* (2004). That album remains by far her biggest seller and most well-known record. Some 20 years on, should you hear a KT Tunstall song on the radio, there is an excellent chance it will be one of those three big hits. In one sense, Tunstall made a rod for her own back by making a debut album that was something of a classic. She saw it as a good problem to have. Although she was under pressure to keep on making commercially successful music, what she did was make very good albums in line with her own creative instincts. Her 2013 release, *Invisible Empire // Crescent Moon*, was both a creative shift and a steep commercial drop-off – a risky moment for an established artist on a major label. But, by that time, KT had already crossed the Rubicon to long-term success. Tunstall has managed to maintain high acclaim all the way to her most recent album, *Nut*, even though that album peaked at a mere 25 in the UK album chart.

Another superstar singer-songwriter, Norah Jones, has followed a similar path. Jones' biggest hits come from her first two albums: three from the phenomenal debut *Come Away With Me* (2002) and one from her sophomore album *Feels Like Home* (2004). Those first two remain her biggest commercial successes (although third album *Not Too Late* also reached number one in both the USA and UK charts). Not only was she the top priority for her record label, Jones became the priority for the whole recording industry – a rare global success in the era of Napster and the height of internet music piracy.

Since then, commercial success has ebbed for Jones, with much lower chart positions for her recent releases. However, those albums were rated highly by critics and fans, despite being a creative departure from the output that brought her early fame. It's this musical evolution that has been so critical to her longevity. As Jones crossed lanes musically, she developed as an artist.

It's worth noting that both KT Tunstall and Norah Jones benefitted from long-standing relationships with their respective record labels: EMI/Virgin and Blue Note. They are both examples of what a productive long-term relationship between artist and label can achieve despite the creative and commercial tug of war experienced by both artists. They demonstrate why labels shouldn't drop artists who want to change creative direction, even if they experience a dip in commercial performance. With great artists, creative and commercial success comes back around (we look at the impact of being dropped by labels next, and it's not what you might expect).

In the streaming era, songs rather than albums have been the music industry's growth engine. Consequently, songwriting has become industrialised on a grand scale. New York-based Hit Songs Deconstructed (which does indeed deconstruct the elements that make a hit song) has reported a steady rise in the number of songwriters per hit. In the year 2000, the average number of songwriters per Billboard Top 10 hit was 2.4. This has increased to four in 2020. Artist services company iMusician analysed the top 100 songs in the UK Official Singles Charts (in June 2023), concluding that it took an average of five songwriters and 2.5 producers to produce a top 40 hit. This is a worry, from the point of view of access for young bands and solo songwriters, who don't have the backing of major labels or publishers and can't afford to attend songwriting camps to cook up hit songs to a tried-and-trusted formula that tickles Spotify's algorithms. Neither KT Tunstall nor Norah Jones ever wrote songs to a formula in the hope of having a hit.

The Future of Hits

The technologization of hits is a phenomenon that has led to rock/indie bands effectively being locked out of the charts. In 2024, *The Rest Is Entertainment* podcast compared the first half of the 80s and 90s with the period 2020–2024. Host Richard Osman found that bands occupied number one in the UK chart for 146 weeks in the first half of the 80s and 141 weeks in the first half of the 90s. Yet during 2020–2024, bands were at number one for three weeks (with one of those being The Beatles' 2023 song "Now and Then"). Bands just can't get on the charts. That may be why many bands of longevity have expressed gratitude to have begun their careers before streaming changed the music industry.

Some attribute the absence of bands from the charts to social media channels that are dominated by individual personalities, leading labels to find and subsequently market solo artists with better results (again, shortcuts). Others suggest changing tastes, such as the dominance of rap, hip-hop, country and pop over genres such as rock and indie, in the past two decades. The economics of the music industry make it a lot harder for bands to become viable (compared to individual artists), too. Rick Beato – our YouTube music guru – traces the problem back to how songs are marketed by major labels and how those songs are written, produced and recorded. Beato assessed the Top 400 global artists on Spotify (based on monthly listeners), finding that only three of the bands featuring on the list were formed within the last ten years – less than one percent of the artists in the top 400. If forming a band is a minor miracle, having success in the music industry with your band is a revelation.

The technologisation of songwriting demonstrates just how important songs have become to a growing industry. Streaming has amplified the importance of hit songs, even if the process for how songs become hits is harder to pin down, with the rise of the 'viral hit' and the murky role of algorithms. Hitmaking will continue to be an essential part of an artist's skill set for as long as we continue to have a music industry, although it looks like the success rate for bands will get even lower as songs are constructed around a formula. Constructing the hit as shortcut to popularity has long tempted songwriters to create something radio friendly (or now, algorithm friendly). Using tried-and-trusted song structures and precision tooled production methods can make modern pop songs less like music and more like ear candy. *The Baffler* writer and author of Spotify critique *Mood Machine* Liz Pelly describes this as "stream bait pop" songs: "Inherently connected to attention, whether it's hard-and-fast attention-grabbing hooks, pop drops and chorus-loops engineered for the pleasure centres of our brains, or music that strategically requires no attention at all – the background music, the emotional wallpaper, the chill-pop-sad-vibe playlist fodder."[7]

With the enormous popularity of 'lean back' or 'focus' music on playlists such as Spotify's *Peaceful Piano*, even the classical world has succumbed to this form of hitmaking. Composers began writing piano pieces made for such playlists, a practice hilariously exposed by the piano and rap star Chilly Gonzales in his song "Neoclassical Massacre".

As social media proliferates, artists now preview their new songs on social media platforms before official release, in an attempt to gain feedback and build buzz around the song. In effect, the viral moment is now coveted *before* release, not after. Things are turning weird, with sped-up songs becoming a trend on TikTok, something no one in the music business predicted. Initially uploaded by users, major labels now release official sped-up, slowed down, reverb and pitched versions of singles alongside original tracks. Streaming services have sped-up songs playlists. Sounds – mere snippets of songs – also trend on TikTok, which the algorithm promotes, making videos more watchable. Artists and labels can now link a sound to a streaming track via TikTok's own distribution platform SoundOn, closing the loop between TikTok and streaming platforms. As we speak, AI technology is enabling the creation

7 *Mood Machine: The Rise of Spotify and the Cost of the Perfect Playlist,* Liz Pelly. Hodder & Stoughton.

of sounds, even wholly generated songs (and, gulp, 'artists') at unprecedented speed and volume. In 2025, Spotify filed a patent for an AI feature that can automatically generate song 'mashups'. The technology will analyse song elements (vocals, instrumental parts, tempo, key, harmony) and combine parts of different songs, to create personalised mashup versions for users. Mashups are not new. Originally (illegally) uploaded by underground mashup creators, EMI adopted the trend and released a compilation, *Mashed*, in November 2007. It took the major label over a year to produce but at the time was a commercial flop and wasn't repeated.

It's hard to determine how much these developments impact listeners' ability to enjoy actual songs, unencumbered by all the tech paraphernalia that comes with them. It may come as a relief to human songwriters and artists that so far, all these rapidly emerging technologies have failed to produce anything that *replaces* genuinely good pop songs. That hasn't stopped AI generating chart hits, however, so who are we to judge? Worryingly, a survey commissioned by Deezer, done by research firm IPSOS in November 2025, reported that 97% of listeners couldn't tell the difference between AI-generated and human-created songs. AI-generated songs, created with minimal or no human input, are flooding streaming services. As this book went to print, Deezer reported some 50,000 AI-generated songs being uploaded onto its service every day (one third of all tracks uploaded onto the service), although the majority are subsequently identified as related to royalty fraud scams. The real concern is what happens when the fraud schemes are removed but 'official' AI tracks begin to land on streaming playlists and are served up by their algorithms (and perhaps even promoted ahead of real songs that cost more for those services to license from labels). Precious discovery and listening slots will get clogged by what is commonly referred to as "AI slop". Yuk. All this means that the stakes are higher for aspiring and emerging bands and artists, now obliged to release their best songs with no idea whether these will rise above the clutter to attract the attention they deserve.

When it comes to written-to-formula hit songs, labels will claim they are responding to consumer trends, what listeners want, and yet listeners often complain how bland music has become and lament the death of "real music". But pop music seems to be in perfectly good health, with new scenes such as hyperpop generating feverish levels of fandom. If songs are under threat from the various alternative technologies, it's hard to explain why country music – the genre of "three chords & the truth" – is seeing a new wave of global superstars drawing bigger audiences than at any time in the history of the genre. However, the more successful the type of song, the more AI will be trained on it. As this book was written, several major US chart hits in the country genre were by AI artists, causing some consternation amongst the country music community. This is happening just as music in general is on the rise culturally, with alternative pop, indie, post-punk and even rock all thriving creatively and making something of a comeback – all driven by the humble vessel of the popular song.

As someone once said, "without songs, we're all just jamming". For artists, the song remains the same – the purest form of communication and rite of passage to an audience. But if your song doesn't make the charts don't worry about it – the only people noticing chart positions these days are record label executives. If when you a play a song live, the crowd draws in and the fans sing the lyrics back to you, keep on playing it and consider it to already be a hit, one that AI can't steal.

ROUTE 2 – GET DROPPED BY YOUR RECORD LABEL

> "Labels, we got you, but do you got us?"
> —Chappell Roan (at the 2025 Grammy Awards)

You read that right. This chapter is called "get dropped by your record label", not get signed by one. Of course, to get dropped, you must first get signed but let's not mess with the narrative thread; being dropped is often the catalyst that spurs artists to do their best work. Evidence of this is abundant.

In February 2002, Danny McNamara, his brother Richard and three friends, Steve Firth, Mickey Dale and Mike Heaton, stepped out on stage to play a sold-out show at London's prestigious Royal Albert Hall. This was a new peak for their band Embrace. They opened that show with the track "Over", probably because they thought it was. Embrace had just been unceremoniously dropped by their record label, Hut (at the time wholly owned by Virgin Records). On Richard's birthday, too. After a phenomenally successful debut album, and despite two further critically acclaimed LPs, Danny McNamara wondered, "Will we ever be here again?"

In the longer run, things turned out for the better. Embrace joined the club of rock and pop artists who have been dropped by their labels, then went on to make their best – and commercially most successful – records. It is somewhat ironic when you consider that, first and foremost, the record label's function is to commercialise music. Often, bands are dropped simply because a record didn't fly, but most of the time, the reasons *why* it didn't remain unresolved. Was it a bad record or bad marketing? A common situation is that an artist's champion within the label (usually the same person who signed them) has gotten fired or moved on elsewhere. Sometimes, as in the case of Embrace, the label went bust. Such events, like the machinations of the music industry in general, are entirely outside of the artist's control.

Mostly, the reason for being dropped is disappointing sales (or streams) – and therein lies the irony when the band goes on to have subsequent and longevous commercial success. Why didn't the label stick with its original thought process and hang on until the next record, when the band will inevitably go on to make something better? If labels can be brutal, they can also be short sighted and sometimes just plain wrong. Meanwhile, artists must be doggedly determined. Although being dropped can be temporarily distressing, and career-wise disorientating, it can also be galvanising. Something happens to artists when judged in that way. They're having none of it, basically. Being in a band is a vocation, not a job. Musicians have a calling. Since they wouldn't consider doing anything else, the only choice after being dropped is to pick yourself up, dust yourself off and get back on the job. But do better next time.

Embrace's fourth album, 2004's *Out of Nothing*, released on new label Independiente, was a reset that took the band back to number one. It also contained the band's only two top ten singles, back in the days when singles were still sold in large numbers on CD. It makes you wonder whether, without the forced adversity, the band would have pulled a rabbit out of the hat in the way that they did. And yes, it did mean that the band signed to another label. Back in 2004, there were far fewer options for self-releasing albums or being a 'DIY' artist. But they found a way. Specifically, they found another true believer in Andy McDonald, Independiente's founder. Of course, Chris Martin of Coldplay famously did them a favour by giving Embrace his song "Gravity", *Out of Nothing*'s lead single. It got the band back in the UK top 10.

Artists dropped by their labels often go on to make their best records, commercially and creatively. This has been the case with a large community of artists, here are a few examples:

- Laura Veirs, dropped by Nonesuch Records after her third album with the label, *Saltbreakers*, and then went on to make *July Flame*, her most successful commercial album (with independent label Bella Union).
- The Wombats, dropped by 14th Floor Records after their third album, *Glitterbug*, then went on to independently release *Beautiful People Will Ruin Your Life*, a number three chart album and huge streaming success.
- Spoon, dropped after their first album release for a major label, *A Series of Sneaks* in 1998, whose next record, *Girls Can Tell*, set them on a course for a glorious run of ten indie-rock albums, including three in the *Billboard* top ten. The band established a long-term relationship with indie label Matador.
- Alela Diane, dropped by Rough Trade after her *Wild Divine* album in 2011, the singer-songwriter went on to forge a successful career releasing albums through independent distributors, leading to her most successful album, *Cusp*.
- Eels, dropped after Dreamworks Records was acquired by Interscope in 2003, went on to make their

masterpiece *Blinking Lights and Other Revelations*, released by another indie label, Vagrant Records, in 2005.

In each case, there was a specific story behind the decisions made, but the overall impression is of short-sighted and rather poor decision making. While being dropped might be bewildering and depressing for the artist, it is important to see it as a new beginning rather than the end. On the other hand, it follows that labels might think twice about dropping artists and perhaps rarely should. Only in extreme cases where all other remedies are exhausted should a hard-won, hard-worked relationship be forced into an abrupt end. From the label's perspective, sticking with an artist that you believed in at the beginning is likely to bear fruit again at some stage – in the above cases, the very next record. Most artists experience creative and commercial highs and lows as a natural ebb and flow – a product of their long-term viability. To accept this requires vision, which is not outside the realm of possibility for a music label, even in these fast-paced times we're living in. In fact, with streaming and social media exacerbating the flood of content and fragmenting of attention spans, the very role of a record label is to bet on those artists who can save the rest of us from merely scrolling ourselves to death. The careers of many artists demonstrate that it can indeed work that way, including the following, for example:

- Norah Jones, who has released 11 studio albums over two decades with Blue Note Records.
- Death Cab For Cutie, in many ways a classic indie band, have released six albums with the major label Atlantic Records over 20 years.

- Real Estate, the New Jersey indie band, have made five albums with Domino Records, a relationship of 15 years.
- Arctic Monkeys, probably the most successful English rock band of modern times, have been with Domino Records since the beginning – seven studio albums across two decades.
- Björk has been with indie label One Little Indian (now One Little Independent) for 11 albums across three decades.
- The National, the indie rock band whose star has steadily ascended from cult status to major festival headliners, have made all 12 of their studio albums with indie label 4AD, over 25 years.

British indie-folk band Fink has been associated with Ninja Tune since the band's first record in 2006. When it became clear that the band's music was something of an outlier compared with that label's core repertoire, instead of ending the relationship, the two entered a long-term partnership under the artist's own imprint, the fabulously named R'Coup'D Records. It allowed Fink's career stability and eventual long-term success, while similar arrangements with other artists have helped Ninja Tune achieve greater scale. A win-win for both the band and the label.

I don't mean to label bash here by the way, that would be too easy and too simplistic. Take the case of Warner Music Group – a few of the labels within Warner are named above, yet the two-decade-long relationship between Atlantic Records and Death Cab For Cutie is exemplary. The record industry is a wreckage site of indie bands that signed to major labels and could not make it work, yet the band is thriving on that label. It was Warner Music and another iconic American indie band, Wilco, that illustrated the idiosyncratic nature of the music business so well in the early 2000s. The band was dropped (Elektra/Reprise) and then effectively re-signed (Nonesuch) by the same label group. Although it has a bizarre angle to it, perhaps this should happen more often – the parent company making more effort to accommodate important artists, albeit in the right label home. Better than letting the band go, surely. Major labels may be huge corporations, but they host truly iconic labels such as RCA, Columbia (Sony Music Group) and Capitol, Island (Universal Music Group), which have long traditions of backing artists over their entire careers, and even occasionally inventing products, like the vinyl album. It would be a shame to see the major labels not live up to their venerable histories.

What is the future for record labels?

Before the streaming era, signing to a label was the first sign of real success for artists. Signing a deal was a heavy hint that you just might make it (even though the common wisdom is that a one in ten chance of sustained success is the best odds you have at that point). Signing to a label meant an income – that huge advance (even if it was a poorly disguised loan). Being signed could bring status and access – to press, radio, TV and importantly, a network of other already successful musicians, producers and songwriters.

Without a doubt, the record label system is due a shake-up. Label executives appear to be fearful for their jobs and burned out, drowning in day-to-day activities and trying to keep up with an endless conveyor belt of priority artists that aren't priorities for very long. And yet, the list of artists who have broken through and then crossed the Rubicon to longevity *without* the help of record labels is extremely short. Attempts to cut out the middleman or, in tech terms, 'disintermediate' the labels, have been launched time and again, only to fizzle out with little trace. Direct-to-fan music platforms like Pledge Music came and went (in the end with some scandal, leaving artists *unpaid*). Patreon, meanwhile, cast the net much wider than musicians and stopped short of offering record label-like marketing services. And Patreon now wants a greater share of revenues, recently hiking its prices. Spotify fancied its chances of going direct at one point, launching Spotify Direct (something of a smoke signal to its label partners) but quickly backed off, leaving labels in a stronger position than at any time since Napster.

The above-mentioned examples of long-term artist-label relationships are testimony to the fact that labels can be partners throughout the whole journey – not just as long as the hits keep coming. With the age of the superstar in relative decline (i.e. fewer household names) and the even greater unpredictability of hits, it is even more important that record labels find a way to build long-term partnerships with artists. The markers of success in the industry are changing, and with it, artists' goals and dreams, which no longer fixate on fame and fortune. Most artists would rather have stable, creative careers that enable them to make a good living doing what they love. They are even willing to turn down that huge advance, having realised they would rather be bootstrapped than up to their eyeballs in debt. At the time of writing, there is an increasing concern across all arts sectors including music, that only those with inherited wealth and privilege can afford to consider pursuing a career in the arts. In July 2025, the UK Government's Creator Remuneration Working Group (CRWG) announced a series of initiatives that the three major labels agreed to implement voluntarily, including a new framework for artists who signed record contracts before streaming (pre-2000) to renegotiate their terms (including writing off unrecouped advances, allowing them to start earning streaming royalties sooner). Major labels also committed to paying songwriters a daily allowance (per diem) of £75, plus expenses, for attending recording sessions, and to increase session musician fees for pop music by up to 40%. These initiatives are a step in the right direction but of course, can go much further. The major labels are making record profits, to the tune of roughly a quarter of one million dollars per hour. To attract the best new talent (if that is what they want to do) there is scope to provide much more financial support in addition to traditional advances and royalties.

Music labels have held an iron grip on the acquisition of talent largely because they put up the money to fund it. Boy George famously said that record labels were "banks where the staff wear jeans". The International Federation of the Phonographic Industry (IFPI) estimates that the music industry invests some $10 billion each year in A&R and marketing – much of it directly in artist advances. However, this is now rapidly changing. Two phenomenal economic success stories, fintech and the creator economy, have now collided. The financing function of labels for new music releases is increasingly being solved by third-party fintech offerings – giving artists an alternative than to take out an expensive label loan. The global fintech market is estimated to be upwards of $200 billion in 2024 (a similar ballpark and range to the creator economy). Artist funding platforms such as Duetti and BeatBread employ AI and predictive analytics to quantify advances to artists based on their streaming and social media profiles. These first-generation fintech players may succeed, but in any event, a second generation is already on the way.

Artist Corporations are a new legal structure being developed specifically for professional creatives, designed to enable artists to set up majority-owned companies that allow them to participate more directly in the capital gains being created in music. Instead of a standard record contract, labels and artists would enter a joint venture, with revenue and profit share arrangements. Artists of ambition have come to realise that a 'traditional' label deal, whereby they hand over their copyright for a considerable term in exchange for an advance, doesn't stack up. Even as artists become entrepreneurs, for them to realise their long-term aspirations and potential, partners are as essential as ever. This may be the age of the 'independent artist' but with the onslaught of technology and the complex challenges it brings to the music industry, artists are more 'interdependent' than ever. Major and independent record labels have a rich history of building careers for music superstars and icons – the ones we know and love. Many rising artists revere these icons and aspire to follow in their footsteps. And yet labels seem to be edging closer to Thom Yorke's prediction of impending disaster. With a perpetual short-term focus and a fixation with TikTok, labels appear to lack the power to create truly original marketing stories, take creative risks with artists or stick with artists and help them develop into legends.

As streaming growth peaks, the majors seem to be making endless rounds of staff cuts, cost reductions and restructuring, inevitably pruning their rosters of any artists not delivering on those all-important streaming spikes. As a result, they are taking fewer risks and not developing talent anything like they used to in the past. The negative stories about creative control, predictability, short-term thinking and worse, mismanagement and abuse, seem to continue with greater frequency than ever. The majors are transforming into vast holding companies, effectively buying their way into the growing 'artist services' space in a global race to grow market share. Universal Music Group acquired two such companies: Ingrooves and PIAS. It has since made a bid to acquire another, Downtown Music Holdings (owner of the ironically named CD Baby). Sony did the same, first with The Orchard and then with AWAL. Acquisition is rapidly becoming the way for the majors to grow.

Major labels have also been busy acquiring music catalogues, buying out superstars for vast amounts of money at peak valuations. Sony acquired the rights for Queen's songs for a record-breaking £1 billion in 2024 and then a similar deal with Pink Floyd saw them commit £400 million. Both Universal and Warner have made similar moves. It seems that these companies now know that their future is in trading established intellectual property portfolios rather than marketing new talent. They have the resources and ability to augment catalogues with new assets such as video, documentary film, podcasts, books and other multi-media rights exploitations. This means AI-assisted modifications such as remasters, remixes and deep catalogue creation. It means investment in archives and the perpetual re-invention of classic, iconic works. They have successfully lobbied for substantial increases to the terms of copyrights in Europe and the USA, laying the groundwork to do just that. Even so, copyrights on music do not last forever.

As the majors peel away from taking bets on new talent, can independent labels thrive by doing a better job of talent acquisition and artist development? The kudos associated with some independent labels remains considerable. Labels like XL (home to Radiohead and Fontaines D.C.) have enormous respect among the artist community. The same goes for ultra-cool indie labels such as JagJaguwar and Dead Oceans. ATO Records, Domino, 4AD, Matador, Cooking Vinyl, Sub Pop, Dirty Hit, Partisan, Ninja Tune, Stones Throw, Merge Records – these are all names that mean something to artists and even fans too in some cases. The indies' weakness remains scale. In an increasingly global marketplace, artists cannot hang around waiting for international success.

Predicting the death of record labels has been a pastime for journalists, industry commentators, futurists, technology gurus and disgruntled artists for a couple of decades now, yet it hasn't come to pass. The leaders and owners of record labels have seen disruptive technologies come and go so many times that they remain unconcerned about any real threat – if they survived internet piracy, they could survive anything. It's a fair point – only labels have the combination of copyright and the ability to take risks on artists at scale – they have become experts at spread betting.

Record labels are not innovators, but they are deceptively good adaptors. They have become much better anticipators of new technologies coming over the horizon. With the emergence of AI, it feels like the labels are prepared and ready to face battles on all fronts – but particularly legal. Many artists, however, are questioning when and if they stand to gain from record companies working out new deals with AI technology platforms. A deal with AI platforms to train technologies on copyrighted music feels like the last deal to be made.

Should today's up-and-coming artists spend time and energy courting labels to become successful? The answer is yes and no. You might sign a record deal to help progress your career to the next level, or you might step up to a major label when you feel you are ready to take your brand global. If you have creative confidence, a fanbase of any size and a clear goal of where you want to go, then labels still make sense. But there is never a need to sign a deal beyond the next project – and so you can enter the relationship with eyes wide open and realistic expectations – not in the hope that you might "make it". That part is now most definitely down to you.

ROUTE 3 – MAKE A CLASSIC ALBUM

> "*OK Computer* is a record that seemed to encapsulate its time (1997), and yet still seems as resonant and relevant today. Radiohead are rare in that they have balanced critical and commercial success for many years, and their most famous offering exemplifies that achievement, enduring analysis at the fingertips of academics even as it exists as background music in coffee bars."
>
> —Tim Footman, author

What is the last classic album to be released? According to Tim Footman, it is Radiohead's *OK Computer*. That's what he wrote in *Radiohead: Welcome to the Machine: OK Computer and the Death of the Classic Album,* published in 2007, a few years before streaming came of age.

Although I don't agree with him, I understand Footman's argument. *OK Computer* is an undeniable classic, achieving the balanced critical and commercial success he describes above. The album introduced Radiohead to a mainstream, global audience and put them firmly on the pedestal of superstardom. It seemed to achieve more than being just a great record, but a collective cultural good – one of those albums everyone knew, bought and had an opinion about. That's really what Footman is driving at with the idea that *OK Computer* may have been the last album (certainly by a rock band) to have achieved that kind of cultural significance and ubiquity. And yet Radiohead's "self-sabotaging" experimental follow-up, *Kid A,* is the album that achieved number one in both the UK and US album charts and set a course for long-term success on the terms the band wanted, not according to anyone else's terms, and certainly not record label expectations. It was *Kid A* that set the tone for Radiohead's subsequent career of creative left turns and rebellion against the establishment of the music business – all of which cemented their legend. Radiohead is the Spartacus of the music scene.

Just two years after *OK Computer* was released, the music industry was plunged into the chaos of the internet piracy era. Napster fuelled a commercial meltdown and the death of the music industry as we knew it then, including the industry's unit of currency, the CD album. Albums were atomised into hundreds of millions of songs, reducing them to drag and drop computer files. Steve Jobs's answer to this music industry cataclysm was to offer individual songs for the breathtakingly reasonable price of 99 cents via the iTunes download store. Then came streaming platforms, completing a seismic shift towards single songs, turning the entire music business into one big "celestial jukebox". The album was repeatedly battered by these massive waves of tech platform dominance. No doubt there have been a string of classic albums each year *since* OK Computer, but they were incrementally less important to the industry than they were the year before, taking up less collective shelf space in peoples' homes.

Yet artists want to make albums, and they also want to make *classic* albums. I have asked many artists the same question: What's best for longevity: a hit single or a classic album? Without exception, artists answer that a classic album matters most. It's ironic, because in the age of digital music i.e. the twenty-first century, while the song has gotten bigger, the role of the album has been called into question many times over. But there is little doubt that many bands of longevity are still powered by albums rather than hit songs. Indeed, so many bands now succeed in building their careers primarily through albums, bands such as The National, Vampire Weekend, Tame Impala and now Fontaines D.C. and Wolf Alice. These bands have made superb albums that hark back to the classic album years, and yet perhaps are not celebrated as such when compared with their equivalents in the pre-digital age. I often think back to the 1990s, an era of complacent music industry growth and bloated CD albums with up to 18 songs, but of a distinctly patchy quality when taken as a whole. Now, we are back to leaner, fitter albums with between eight and 12 songs, distinctive sides (thanks to the vinyl resurgence) and strong coherent themes. All killer no filler. And yet there is also a strong sense that these albums come along with such frequency that they quickly evaporate and do not have the same legacy of albums made before… *OK Computer*. I put this to Martin Courtney, lead singer and main songwriter of another 'album band', New Jersey's Real Estate, asking "is it still possible to make a classic album these days?". His response was: "Well, you can *make* one, but the question is, will anybody notice?".

The Coral is a band revered on the music scene – a real band's band. They are a group of accomplished musicians who first got together at school in the small Wirral town of Hoylake. The band members bonded over their many music icons, from The Beatles and the Small Faces to Acker Bilk and Del Shannon. Listening to a record by The Coral is a dizzying mix of Liverpool's music hall pop heritage together with American West Coast psychedelia and a lot else besides, all the while sounding like no other band except The Coral. The band has had a few brushes with mainstream success but were never comfortable with it. They had three singles in the UK top ten, notably the 2003 top five hit "Pass It On". When the band was elevated to the top of Britpop mania in 2002 with their song "Dreaming of You" and a Mercury Music Prize-nominated debut album, they had a great time basking in the limelight while upending industry etiquette (a Freddie Mercury impersonator stood in for them at the Mercury Prize ceremony).

But albums are The Coral's speciality. The band have had six top ten albums and have become unlikely experts in riding the music industry rollercoaster. Just as the band hit their stride, founding member and guitarist Bill Ryder-Jones quit. The band had reached a critical juncture and didn't feel they could replace him. Instead, a change of sound and style, by necessity, brought them another critically revered record, *Distance Inbetween* (2016). Despite no further chart success with singles, the band became a respected going concern with a solid fanbase. Two albums later, they released their masterpiece, *Coral Island*. In 2023, The Coral followed up with two companion albums, again thematically based, the "surreal Italian spaghetti western soundtrack" *Sea of Mirrors* and the vinyl-only LP *Holy Joe's Coral Island Medicine Show* – a rough sequel to *Coral Island*. The Coral seem destined to make interesting and highly rated records for as long as they wish to carry on working and yet they haven't had a bona fide chart single for two decades.

Another band that emerged from the Wirral, before members of The Coral were even born, is Orchestral Manoeuvres in the Dark, also known as OMD. After an early top ten single, "Messages", their star ascended with UK number three chart single "Enola Gay" from their second album *Organisation*. Then came an early masterpiece album, *Architecture & Morality*. To say the album was creatively ambitious is an understatement. OMD brought in choral samples, a Mellotron, and shockingly for fans, guitars. The album's nine songs blended the experimental and commercial to make up an accessible but avant-garde concept album (the title was taken from the book *Morality and Architecture* by David Watkin). *Architecture & Morality* became OMD's biggest commercial success, reaching number three on the UK Albums Chart and achieving top ten across much of Europe. It has been recognised as a seminal album of its era and a timeless synth-pop classic, often appearing in "greatest of all time" lists, including the publication *1001 Albums You Must Hear Before You Die*. OMD have staged multiple tours based around the album. Even after building fame as a 'singles band', the album format remains OMD's principal vehicle for storytelling and artistic expression. OMD's 2017 album *The Punishment of Luxury* is arguably one of the band's best, made forty years after they first got together. The band's 2023 album *Bauhaus Staircase* marks a continuation of OMD's relationship with both music and art, with a strong conceptual connection to design movements like Bauhaus. Lead singer and bass guitarist Andy McClusky describes the importance of albums: *"It's the craftsmanship involved in making albums. Our most iconic records, like* Architecture & Morality, *were the result of us building soundscapes before melodies. That shows how integral the process [of making an album] is to creating something truly lasting."*

What is the future for the album?

Music industry infrastructure lags technology and consumer trends, not least when it comes to albums. In a recent conversation this author had with a UK major record label head, I was told "artists still want to make albums, but we don't really know what to do with albums any more". For an extensive deep dive into the album's resurgence, see my book *Body of Work: How the Album Outplayed the Algorithm.* The album has been remarkably resilient in the song-dominated era of playlist culture and music streaming. Many in the music business predicted that streaming would weaken, even kill off, the album format. The thinking was that in the engagement model of streaming, artists would instead be better off releasing a constant flow of single tracks – in other words, a constant reminder to fans not to forget about them. In any case, listeners would no longer have the attention spans to cope with whole albums. Spotify was even presumptuous enough to make "shuffle play" the default mode for albums, until Adele intervened, insisting this was removed on the release of her 2021 album *30*. She tweeted at the time: *"This was the only request I had in our ever-changing industry! We don't create albums with so much care and thought into our track listing for no reason. Our art tells a story, and our stories should be listened to as we intended. Thank you, Spotify, for listening."*

Contrary to any expectations at the start of the century, the album is now a stronger format than ever. *Billboard* recently surmised that "In truth, the demise of the album was probably exaggerated in the first place", but I'm not so sure. The album survived Napster and internet piracy, the short-lived reign of iTunes, the dominance of streaming and even the ubiquity of social media and the age of short-form content.

The album held on and now thrives, for a combination of the following reasons:

- Artists – almost every one of whom continue to want to make albums. The album is the perfect vessel for the art of making songs and artists know that albums are where all good songs come from. An album is the book, while the song is merely a chapter. As super-producer and music artist Jack Antonoff (Bleachers) told the *And The Writer Is…* podcast, "There's no brilliant artist that hasn't existed for a real period of time and changed things and has a real audience that isn't based on albums. They don't exist."

- Vinyl – without the vinyl resurgence, I doubt the album would have held on to its purpose. Albums remain the currency of the physical music business, and in many markets, including the USA and UK, the rate of growth of vinyl sales has outpaced streaming. With younger demographics now embracing vinyl culture, this growth is much more than the nostalgia-driven niche the music industry first assumed. Owning the vinyl LP has become an expression of fandom and a symbol of support for the artist.
- The music industry – Record Store Day, The Grammys, and in the UK The BRITS, Mercury Music Prize and National Album Day all shore up the album concept and have helped brick & mortar record shops not just survive but grow into a vibrant retail sector. The music industry kept on measuring "album sales" even when there was no such thing in the streaming age and still nobody knows how much album listening really happens. But album charts still exist and still matter to artists and labels putting out new albums.

Safe to say, the album's future looks secure. The album's future is *exciting*. As I put it in *Body of Work*:

> Artists aspire to see their work in the album format. Indeed, I've yet to come across an artist that doesn't appreciate albums and the idea of seeing their work come to life as an expression of this art form — a statement of where they are creatively at a point in time and a stage in their career and life. The opportunity to add to the legacy, the canon, the oeuvre.

For artists, the album is an artistic quest – a chance to demonstrate what you are capable of. And although it is perhaps harder than ever to achieve, your next album might even become celebrated as a classic.

ROUTE 4 – ACHIEVE CULT STATUS, AKA QUIET LEGEND

"I like my audience small but loyal. I don't need to be on a lunchbox to feel successful."
—Tom Waits (as told to *Spin* magazine in 1988)

It's not a new debate, but like you, I often wonder who the music legends of tomorrow will be. Which of today's artists can stand on the shoulders of giants? Will London's Wolf Alice blossom into something momentous, like Radiohead? Could Dublin's Fontaines D.C. become modern heirs to U2? Could Essex rock band Nothing But Thieves be a Led Zeppelin for the streaming age? Is Sam Fender a potential successor to Springsteen? You might think these examples are unlikely, and maybe rightly. In my conclusion to this book, I take a quick dive into these artists – all British or Irish – to make my own brief assessment.

The music business and modern culture have changed too much for any band or artist to hold ambitions to be 'the best in the world'. The top slots are taken. Taylor Swift isn't going anywhere. With over 250 million songs on streaming platforms and approximately 99,000 songs a day uploaded (that is the estimate by music measurement firm Luminate, *before* AI-generated tracks are included). Each time an artist or band releases a record, they are competing for attention with an impossible quantity of choices for every single music listener. The music industry is a competitive world of unfair advantages where talent does not rise naturally to the top. The music industry is purposefully designed to make artists compete with one another. The charts – still a central obsession for major label marketers – are pure competition. Getting onto a playlist is a scrum for precious slots – again, a competition. TikTok virality may appear more random in nature, but the multiple efforts to tickle its algorithm into responding is a competition of a different form, more akin to a gold rush. For artists, it can feel like songs are entry tickets into a music lottery, with the odds of winning not dissimilar to an actual lottery.

The thing with competitions is that most entrants are set up to fail. So, if you don't make the charts or get on a playlist with your latest release or get an award nomination this year, you have de facto 'failed'. Certainly, you will have disappointed your label reps, who will now find it that much harder to pitch you to media and streaming platforms but also internally – to get precious time from marketers and continued patience from company bosses. Again, the competition within the label system is to become a 'priority artist'. The competitive nature of the music industry can make artists feel like they are not as good as they truly are.

Setting goals in this environment can seem futile, so much being outside the artist's control. Yet every artist needs some form of validation. The good news is that achieving success on the artist's terms, outside of mainstream industry expectations, is a long-standing music tradition of the so-called 'cult-artist'. Many cult-status artists initially found fandom through smaller, niche audiences and underground music scenes. In the book *Our Band Could Be Your Life: Scenes from the American Indie Underground, 1981–1991* by Michael Azerrad, whole careers are mapped out through the alternative underground college radio scenes, in which bands such as Minutemen, Black Flag, Mission of Burma, Hüsker Dü and The Replacements are immortalised. Some of them, like Sonic Youth and Dinosaur Jr. continue to thrive, their cultural cache rising steadily over time. That's the sweet spot for cult bands, attracting devoted fans who feel a deep connection to their work and gaining recognition with new generations.

In a review for UK band Tindersticks' 2024 album *Soft Tissue, The Guardian*'s chief music critic, Alexis Petridis, wrote: *"There was a brief moment where it looked as if the Nottingham band's lushly orchestrated, emotive songs might find a wide audience. But they were doomed to remain a critically acclaimed cult concern… Yet in a sense, that cult status has served them well in their second act."*

Indeed it has. Tindersticks have lasted 33 years (albeit with a five-year hiatus) and made 13 studio albums, with most of them lauded by critics and much-loved by their dedicated fanbase. Only their second album, *Tindersticks* (referred to as "the second Tindersticks album", since both it and their debut were self-titled – a fitting quirk for a cult band) reached anything like commercial success, making number 13 in the UK album chart. Only one of the band's singles has made the UK top 40 ("Bathtime" in 1997 reached the lofty heights of number 38). And yet 30 years on, *Soft Tissue* is among their best work, and the band included London's prestigious Royal Albert Hall in its 2025 tour. While music writers still associate cult status with words such as "doomed", bands have moved on. Cult status is something to aspire to.

Scottish rock band Teenage Fanclub are another cult group who have barely troubled the charts when it comes to singles (having crept into the UK top 20 just once). However, they have had five top 20 albums, all of them critically revered. When Teenage Fanclub formed in 1989, times were hard for traditional guitar-based rock music. It was pre-grunge, pre-Britpop, and the charts were still in the grip of mass-produced pop. Yet, something was afoot across the musical axis of the Eastern Seaboard, Seattle (Washington) and *Glasgow*. The peak of Sonic Youth, Dinosaur Jr., Yo La Tengo, The Jesus and Mary Chain, The Vaselines… and very much arriving at that time, Teenage Fanclub. They were at the very beginning of the resurgence of guitar music – the era of Creation Records and Oasis, Sub Pop and Nirvana – a decade of legend-making stories in which "The Fannies" played a series of important cameos.

The band never formed an attachment to music industry badges of success. They are self-deprecating Scots who considered themselves to have achieved their dream just by releasing an album (*A Catholic Education*, 1990). Yet 35 years on, they are as loved as ever by their fans, as well as lots of other musicians. The Fannies achieved longevity without a hit song or streaming success but are considered influential by many subsequent indie guitar bands to emerge on both sides of the Atlantic in the twenty-first century.

Bands such as Tindersticks and Teenage Fanclub have given cult bands a good name. A cult band is no longer a euphemism for some level of 'failure'. Nor is it something to settle for. Cult status is what most bands now strive for. Cult bands are often credited with inventing new genres. Arizona band Calexico has a cult status that make Teenage Fanclub look like a boy band. Joey Burns, John Convertino and bandmates have had one song on the UK top 100, but a dozen critically revered albums over three decades. None of the band's top Spotify songs are from any of those albums. They are a cover version (*Alone Again Or*, originally by the band Love from their classic 60s album, *Forever Changes*), a movie soundtrack, a Christmas song and a collaboration with indie folk artist Iron & Wine. Calexico's repertoire is a unique hybrid of Latin styles crossed with Americana that sounds like nobody else – so much so that music writer Fred Mills created a new genre to describe it: "desert noir".

In recognition of its validity, I suggest renaming cult status as "quiet legend". My advice to bands is not to waste time trying to conform to music industry expectations but instead focus on creating a world which you and your fans can occupy and develop together. This idea of 'world building' is much more appealing than constantly striving to make 'the numbers', impressing gatekeepers or becoming enslaved to social media platforms. It requires a singular focus on musical style, compelling live performance and patient building of a song catalogue that will draw fans in for the long haul. There are many examples of bands that have taken this approach.

Montreal's Half Moon Run blends folk, rock, indie and electronic elements in a way that defies typical categorization. The band's music is textured, introspective and layered – a product of the trio's musical virtuosity that doesn't fit neatly into mainstream pop trends or algorithm-driven playlists. How can a band with no hits, non-charting albums and an unmemorable name thrive in today's music scene? Being brilliant helps, but the band built a foundation by touring extensively, opening for bigger bands and playing festivals, knowing they could win audiences over with impressive live performances. The band has grown creatively with each album, their fourth, *Salt*, garnering the best reviews of their career. Half Moon Run clearly have an evolving creative vision that hasn't been distracted by trying too hard to please. Even in their use of social media, the band communicates a sense of something classic, making effective use of photography and video especially in capturing their live shows and musical prowess. Just over a decade into their career, the band has already reduced its reliance on industry expectations and leaned into its relationship with fans instead.

Toronto's Metric arrived at the turn of the twenty-first century in New York City to join a hot scene of indie-rock that included The White Stripes, The Strokes, Interpol and Yeah Yeah Yeahs. According to Metric's lead singer, keyboardist and songwriter, Emily Haines: "Invisibility is important to the idea [of not having a hit record] in that it is foundational." In other words, it gives you time to hone your craft and keep improving on your own terms. Metric's first few albums are the sound of a band finding its range. Then, the band's fourth album *Fantasies* (2009) found its target; a perfect mix of everything they had done before but with more confident songwriting and production. Even better, *Fantasies* was self-released and wholly owned by the band, not a record label. Back in 2009 this was a trailblazing move which paid off handsomely. After many years of struggle and some false starts, Metric went platinum in Canada with *Fantasies*. And that was that – the Rubicon to longevity was crossed in the best possible way, with a classic, and wholly independent album. From there Metric has become one of those bands that have paved the way for independence as self-releasing copyright-owning pioneers.

It's not just Canadian bands. My favourite example of quiet legend comes from Scotland. Glasgow post-rock band Mogwai's output spans 11 studio albums (plus several accomplished soundtracks) over 30 years. They never consciously planned for their success, or for longevity, as songwriter and guitarist Stuart Braithwaite made clear: *"I don't see any of this as conscious… We weren't expecting to be making five/six albums, never mind ten or 11."* Despite the resolute lack of planning, Braithwaite and his band have become masters of the music long game. Their first album to reach the UK top 40 chart was *Mr Beast* (2006), and since then, each subsequent album has found a wider audience than the last. Bearing in mind, much of this was under their own steam, too. With their own label, Rock Action Records, launched in 2010, Mogwai have no one else to please except themselves and no bosses other than their fanbase.

What is the future for cult artists?

The future for cult artists is great! Indeed, cult artists really are the future of the music industry. Cult status used to be music's consolation prize, very much second best. Cult artists had either had a shot at fame and missed, or just never got accepted by the establishment. In other words, rejects. But now, cult status is highly desirable. The music business is not the mass-market monoculture that its 'star maker' mentality was founded on. Instead, it has become a sprawling, interconnected web of small but passionate communities, sub-cultures and evolving music scenes. This has been a tough transition for music labels, but for cult artists, it's more of an opportunity than a threat.

Artists of cult status can thrive without ever relying on the music industry to turn them into stars. As we've discussed, many artists were never comfortable with stardom anyway. These days, most modern bands and music artists function more like cult acts, in the sense that they cultivate deeply engaged, small audiences rather than striving for fame. The intensity and loyalty of a cult following is something most artists would happily trade with size.

Streaming platforms enable limitless real estate for artist music catalogues, and this has led to more artists than ever finding sustainable audiences, even if each fan base is relatively small. Cult bands can thrive in this environment because they no longer need traditional music promotion, but a patient building of word-of-mouth, harnessing many of the dynamics of Kevin Kelley's "1,000 true fans" theory (think small not large, depth not breadth, a direct relationship with fans). Cult artists excel at this model because their audiences are emotionally invested, not passive consumers. Platforms such as Bandcamp, Patreon, Substack and Discord allow artists to cultivate their fan base and encourage their fans to act as sponsors and advocates. Emergent platforms such as Subvert, Elastic Stage and Artist Corporations are designing their purpose around cult artists and niche creators.

Cult status doesn't always mean small. Cigarettes After Sex, Beach House, Men I Trust and Khruangbin all progressively built on cult status to notch up millions of monthly streaming listeners and slowly transform into global touring bands. Their brand of cult status optimises streaming platforms in that they have benefitted from playlists, algorithmic promotion and the global nature of audiences.

Cult status takes time to build. However, it can be developed co-operatively with audiences. Occasionally asking your fan base three simple questions can act as a guide and compass to keep on building your world, cult status or quiet legend:

1. Which album is your favourite?
2. What songs do you want us to play live?
3. What would you like us to do more of? (songs, albums, merch, live shows, videos, social media content).

The answers to these simple questions will drive an even stronger bond between you and your fans.

ROUTE 5 – TURN THE BAND INTO A B®AND

"We're never gonna be a huge band and I don't care"
—Chino Moreno, of Deftones (as quoted on Blabbermouth.net, 2006)

I love the above quote because as the Californian alternative rock band Deftones continued to progress, they indeed became huge. The band has over 17 million monthly listeners on Spotify and an army of fans that enable Deftones to sell out world tours. For a rock band in the streaming age, Deftones have become as big as it gets. In doing so they have brought their genre – a heady mix of nu metal, shoegaze (and therefore, 'nu gaze'), hardcore and a few other styles - to a wider audience. Is Deftones also a brand? Most definitely. The band has a strong, recognizable image, including the distinctive fonts used for the band's logo. They curate their own festival. They engage in commercial activities like merchandise collaborations. Deftones' most recent collaboration with apparel brand Dickies was an instant, phenomenal success. The line of hoodies, T shirts and sweatshirts, launched at the band's own Dia De Los festival, sold out on release in November 2025. It wasn't something crudely put together, the two brands had a long-running and fascinating relationship. Frontman Chino Moreno often wore Dickies workwear in the band's early years, making the brand part of their iconic 90s look. This spurred bootleg merch and a dispute between the band and Dickies, resulting in a cease and desist notice at one point. Decades later the two have realised it makes sense to collaborate. It's an example of what all brands strive to be; creative and authentic. Deftones have developed a strong and distinct brand identity around their music and culture and that has been key to the band's path to becoming huge, as unlikely as that seemed to Moreno in 2006. It's not a cynical commercial strategy to extract money from fans, but it does use all the band's creative elements in a way that makes Deftones more attractive to fans beyond their music. Fans are buying into the culture Deftones is creating, literally.

No longer anathema to artists and bands, branding has become more important than ever. To stand out from the mass of competition, bands would do well to set out with a mission statement and apply the classic brand discipline of integrated marketing communications: clear consistent messaging, displaying a set of values or themes, having a consistent visual look and feel, including a distinctive font – just like Deftones. If this sounds mercenary, it doesn't have to be. Many of the disciplines of branding come more naturally to cultural phenomena like rock bands than they do commercial products: a cool name, an artisan product, a sonic and visual message and a clear sense of purpose. Many corporate brands could learn more from well-branded rock bands than vice versa. The most important word in branding is authenticity, and bands have an authenticity that most brand product managers would kill for. Branding helps bands and artists manage many facets of the modern music industry with a greater element of control, not least social media. Maintaining a social media presence can be a chore for artists, but lending some clever branding to your socials can give it much more purpose. Succeeding in the music business has never been just about the music, and that applies more now than ever.

When Irish post-punk band Fontaines D.C. returned with their fourth album *Romance*, they embraced image in a way many bands in the genre had hitherto been avoiding, including Fontaines themselves. It helped. The classic look of the Gen Z rock band had been 'anti-fashion', with the t-shirt its principal uniform. Fontaines fashioned up. The band realised that styling is a factor, and their new look was described by music and culture writer Rachel Aroesti as "an amalgam of shiny sportswear, nu-metal jean chains, Keith Flint-style cyberpunk and grungy androgyny" (along with the odd Thin Lizzy t-shirt as a nod to their Dublin roots). With the band stepping up to bigger live venues and festival slots, switching record labels and expanding their sound, the *Romance* project required them to lean into the idea of being a b®and. For the *Romance* artwork and cover concept, the band licensed a series of works by Taiwanese artist Lulu Lin, which brought striking visuals to the project. The band's Instagram was transformed, along with their stage look, tour posters and media presence. They are reinventing the idea of a band of *nonchalance* and doing a superb job of it.

B®ands are more than the sum of their parts. A b®and is more likely to carry on even after a key member moves on, or the band is hit by some other music industry missile. One of the best examples of a b®and is New York band Interpol. Interpol have honed their craft over 20 years since they blasted onto the scene in 2002 with *Turn On the Bright Lights* (one of those infamous "overnight success" records that was really the product of five years of hard graft). Interpol has experienced every phase of the classic longevity curve of a rock band: the much-hyped debut album; the adventure with major labels and global stardom (and then being dropped); the madness of the rock & roll lifestyle; the loss of a founding member (bassist Carlos Dengler left in 2009) and the realisation that the music industry isn't all it's cracked up to be.

Interpol's use of font, colour, image and artwork communicates an aesthetic that perfectly decorates the band's music. They perform live in sharp, black suits, while red, white, black and grey underpin the visual of each of their albums. The band licensed a Garry Winogrand photograph for the cover of 2015 album *Marauder*, while the cover of 2022's *The Other Side of Make-Believe* is Tim Head's photograph (of a razorblade) *Equilibrium*. The band's *éclat* allows such cool choices. Since Interpol came on the scene, everything about the music industry has changed, yet the band has built a distinctive and sturdy brand that allows them to do whatever they want. No wonder that Bowie was an Interpol fan.

A band's brand can extend to their politics. The Manic Street Preachers fans love the band's politics almost as much as their music. Pearl Jam fans admire the band's stance against many facets of the music industry, including ticket prices and dubious business practices in the live music business. Pearl Jam have gone much further into politics with active campaigning. In the 2020 US presidential elections, Frontman Eddie Vedder posted a step-by-step guide on how to vote by mail on his Instagram page.

Perhaps no other band has taken branding further than American heavy rock band KISS (and perhaps they took it too far). Their stage makeup, comic character personas and over-the-top theatrical performances created something unique in rock. Over the past decade, KISS took merchandise to a whole new level by including action figures, comic books, pinball machines, *coffins* and a KISS-themed cruise. Despite their recent retirement from live performance, they have no ambitions to stop the branding blitz. Indeed, they recently converted their brand into cash, selling their song catalogue, name, image and likeness rights (including face-paint designs) to music investment firm Pophouse Entertainment, in a deal reported to be worth more than $300 million. Pophouse's vision is to preserve KISS's "iconic music, enigmatic personas and expressive imagery for generations to come". That starts with a 2027 tour, to feature virtual avatars created by Industrial Light & Magic, a project with a rumoured investment of some $200 million.

The ultimate b®and must count as one of music's coolest inventions – the Ramones. Every original member of Ramones is now dead and yet their brand lives on. The band's logo (a send up of the presidential seal) is now a timeless fashion symbol worn on t-shirts by people who may never have heard *Blitzkrieg Bop*. Their image – ripped jeans, leather jackets, white canvas sneakers and (invariably) shades, is genuinely iconic. The (entirely unrelated) band members all took the same last name, and so Ramones became a family to the outside world, complete with legendary 'family' bust-ups. No wonder Ramones became punk archetypes. As Jeff Tweedy lovingly writes:

> As for the songs themselves, it's hard to pick just one. And in a way, individually, they don't matter. Favourites aside, what matters is the travail – the discipline and gargantuan levels of self-possession required to create not just a 'band' with 'songs' but to invent a world where every gesture is iconic[8].

8 *World Within a Song*, Jeff Tweedy. Faber & Faber.

Creating a b®and isn't a gimmick but a solid foundation for success. So much of music marketing now relies on pushing a series of buttons without knowing which one will work. Organic social posts, paid social ads, playlists, pitching influencers – some of it sticks and some of it doesn't. However, with every song release, the same buttons are pushed again, and on it goes.

A band needs more than that to stand out from the crowd, hence the reason branding is becoming more important to artists. You need a *story* – to build continuity and eventually, to build your myth.

What is the future for b®ands?

In Jarvis Cocker's autobiographical *Good Pop Bad Pop*, Cocker revealed how he had plotted Pulp's image and how the band would "change music as we know it", when he was still a teenager:

> The group shall work its way into the public eye by producing fairly conventional, yet slight off-beat, pop songs. After gaining a well-known and commercially successful status the group can then begin to subvert and restructure both the music-business and music itself.

Cocker's ambitions may have fallen short when it came to restructuring the entire music business, but as one of the founding fathers of Britpop and much else besides, his vision was fully executed (see also longevity themes part 1: The Manifesto).

Brand building is much more than running a marketing campaign or plugging away at a variety of promotion tactics. It takes considerable creative thought, forward planning and meticulous attention to detail. That's why in recent years, bands, managers and labels have turned to creative agencies to do branding and marketing for them, in the hope that they bring some fresh ideas. But artists themselves may have the best ideas. British music collective SAULT create an ultra-cool blend of R&B, contemporary gospel, hip-hop and pop. The project is helmed by songwriter and producer Inflo, but includes vocalists Cleo Sol, Kid Sister and Chronixx, plus other regular collaborators. The group frequently puts Black-centric issues to the foreground, while the band themselves remain so far in the background that their members were anonymous for the first few album releases. As a way of cutting through the clutter, SAULT is a hugely successful b®and.

A b®and can help nurture the fan loyalty so crucial to sustainability and longevity. Kentucky band My Morning Jacket have embraced this idea, building their own fan community around the concept of 'One Big Family'. What marketers used to call a brand extension, One Big Family was created from the kernel of one of the band's early songs, "One Big Holiday". The song became a firm fan favourite and was itself adopted as the name for My Morning Jacket's own independent live festival events. Via One Big Family, fans are first to receive news, notifications on forthcoming shows, product offers and releases, and they can share content around topics set by the band members. To some extent, One Big Family has restored band leader Jim James' faith in the music business itself, as he told me on *The Art of Longevity*:

> It is so amazing, such a blessing. How lucky are we that there is this group of people that want to see us play and will travel to see us play. You see this thing growing and hear about friendships forming over the band – it brings

our world so much more life and so much more joy. That energy goes right back into us.

My Morning Jacket are just one example of bands that have been re-inventing the concept of the fan club by growing a community beyond their social media following. The National, Placebo, Radiohead and others have used direct-to-fan methods and their own fan clubs to forge a much deeper relationship with their fans, with authenticity and informality central to everything they do.

Solo artists have other options. A few established artists, Jeff Tweedy and Laura Marling among them, have turned to Substack or their own web pages as the primary way to communicate with their fans. Nick Cave's *Red Hand Files* (Cave answers fan questions in his unique style) strengthens the bond with his fan community and has undoubtedly contributed to Cave's own creative journey.

These types of connection between artists and fans have previously been obstructed by layers of industry – labels, retailers, distributors, PR and press. For artists, an essential part of the job is to work alongside these traditional music business layers but also navigate around them and build a direct line to fans. Artists are placing themselves at the centre of fan building strategies, whatever their career stage. From the 'Neil Young Archives', to Eryka Badu's 'Badu World Market' and the 'Radiohead Public Library', there are more examples that offer deeper fan experiences or more direct commercial opportunities for artists.

Why should the tech bros end up making all the money? After all, your band is a way cooler brand than the means of distribution, isn't it?

PART 3

20 LESSONS IN LONGEVITY

Not all artist careers fit the outline of Brett Anderson's "stations of the cross" theory, but almost all recognise the narrative. The 'struggle' is a part of the career of just about every musician under the sun, a rite of passage. And yet, once success comes, it is often positioned (by the music industry) as overnight – the result of one hit song, or a stroke of marketing genius. The reality is that this big moment is really the result of a struggle towards some kind of recognition. The blow-up artists of 2024, Chappell Roan and Sabrina Carpenter, had both been working solidly for 10 years. There were few equivalents in 2025 – despite the huge array of new talent in music, the industry cannot suddenly conjure up a new superstar. They are either there and ready to blow, or not. Music careers are not linear, and longevity requires embracing the ebb and flow – both creative and commercial, two ever fluctuating curves that occasionally intersect.

But crossing the Rubicon is real. Artists strongly connect with the concept of 'reaching the other side', a relative utopia where you are no longer at the mercy of 'the industry'. No more trying to please gatekeepers, no attachment to music industry merit badges - just you, your music and your fans. Some artists cross the Rubicon to long-term success shortly after the first peak of fame – propelled forward by a string of hits. Others get there after being unceremoniously dropped by their labels and then bouncing back with their best work. Some artists make a big impression with a standout album. Others arrived the long way around – the slow-burn route of cult success – album-by-album, tour-after-tour. Others steadily build on their brand to hit new creative heights, make a cultural impact and break through to a wider audience. Most are grateful to labels and the industry for the initial surge of resources and whatever tactics were employed on their behalf, while others found a way to make themselves famous, never relying on the industry to do it for them. It's a marathon not a sprint, and when up & running, I'm suggesting a pro-active agenda, by way of 20 lessons (or themes) for longevity, as illuminated across the various episodes *of The Art of Longevity* podcast. The aim is to equip aspiring artists and creators with an element of foresight, knowing and awareness.

If you are the artist, the themes are in no particular order and should not be taken literally but dipped into as a guide or inspiration. If you are the fan, these themes will provide an insight into the mind's eye of the artist as they navigate the tricky territory of the music business. Next time you put on your favourite record by any of these artists – or any others you count yourself a fan of – consider the provenance of the work you are listening to. It reached you through a system so complex and subject to chance, you might see the songs and albums for what they are – minor miracles. By all means stream them but get into vinyl (or cassette or CD) and buy the albums. Go to the shows and buy the t-shirt. Even better, join the fan club or the cult. And when you discover a new artist you love, tell your friends to do the same. That way, these new artists stand a better chance of becoming tomorrow's legends.

To break down the 20 themes, there are three categories as follows:

1. The manifesto. Themes about setting up for success and cementing a belief system that will see you through.
2. Mastering the craft. Themes about the work itself. Graft, focus, collaboration, detail, openness to ideas and reducing distractions.
3. Managing expectations. Themes about the subjective nature of success, staying connected to what you do and why you do it.

Within each category and for each theme, there are some examples and inspiring quotes drawn from the podcast.

THEME 1 – THE MANIFESTO

One of the fastest rising bands on the UK music scene is The Last Dinner Party, now two albums into a promising career. Before they had rehearsed or toured, the London-based five piece committed to a vision of what kind of band they wanted to be. The band's vocalist Abigail Morris and bassist Georgia Davies wrote the manifesto during a night out, on a cheap notepad. It contained the words *decadence*, *gothic* and *indulgent*, and included notes on colours and choice of fabrics for the band's wardrobe.

A manifesto is like a mission statement, but better. The word manifest hasn't become popular without reason. The word aligns with the idea of intentionally bringing desires, goals or visions into reality. The manifesto is the self-delusion of the would-be pop star made real. You don't necessarily have to write it down, although that might help, even on a cheap notepad. While the music business isn't the place for making long-term plans, it certainly is the place for lasting principles, i.e. having some. A central set of ideas that you can return to should you get distracted or get led astray.

The manifesto forms the core values at the heart of your brand. It means you know what you're about and the path you're on. This is a wholly impressive thing to get across to those who might otherwise bend your ear. If you have a strong band leader, they will already have the manifesto plotted out –

either in notebooks or in their heads – with every detail including how you will look, who will design your album covers and how you will change the music business once you make it big (see Jarvis Cocker's earlier quote).

Get on board with the manifesto and it will power you through the early part of your career – maybe all the way to long-term success. Here are a few ideas along these lines.

1. Make art not entertainment

Neil Hannon's band The Divine Comedy (Irish singer-songwriter Hannon *is* the band) perhaps never quite made the A-list of the 1990s British music boom. His journey was not that of Suede, or even kindred spirits, Pulp, but, as The Divine Comedy, Hannon still had three 'ironclad years' of full-on fame after the top 10 UK chart hit "The National Express" in 1999. But Britpop's peak was long gone, and big beat, emo rock and boy band pop had taken over the charts. After a creative left turn (the 2001 album *Regeneration* was a decent attempt at Radiohead-style indie-rock), The Divine Comedy hit a career buffer. Labels, music press and audiences turned lukewarm, leaving Hannon with a problem to solve:

> I went back to the source. I'm going to make a record that makes me happy and no one else. It got me back on course. It wasn't plain sailing, but it was a lot easier after that. To know that this is what I do, and you don't have to go looking for a public, they will come to you.

Beirut, from Sante Fe, New Mexico is both a full band and sometimes the solo vehicle of Zach Condon. The band's early albums (*Gulag Orkestar*, 2006, *The Flying Club Cup*, 2007) were unique, the product of Condon's musical obsessions at the time: Balkan Brass, French Chanson and some mariachi thrown into the mix for good measure. Later on, Condon stripped back those styles somewhat on albums such as *The Riptide* and *No No No*, which both contained a set of catchy songs with strong melodies. This mix of unique style and catchy tunes is why Beirut's songs have found their way onto playlists and done well on streaming platforms. Condon is both amused and bemused by this. But then his entire career has avoided following music industry conventional forms. Instead, his manifesto was to commit to an alternative route.

> I've always felt that I stood right outside the river. The music industry is this river and it's always flowing in this direction and there are all these people that are part of it, moving along with it. And I'm outside it, but somehow I've made my living and I've found my audience.

Of course, the true goal for artists is to make music that works effectively as both art *and* entertainment. We return to our "honorary professor of longevity", Chilly Gonzales, who eloquently puts it:

> The best works of art will always function on a superficial level that brings you in – everybody is on the same page now – we are all trying to succeed by having a catchy song that can live on 20 second snippets on TikTok but artists who are doing it at the highest levels are still managing to sneak in a deeper artistic meaning or holding up a mirror to society. Billie Eilish, Chappell Roan or Melanie Martinez…you can tell their goal is for their music to exist on both levels.

The American playwright Thornton Wilder once said "If you write to impress it will be bad, but if you write to express it will be good." Many artists have gotten bogged down by either trying to write a hit or trying to write a song like the one that previously was a hit. This is made harder by the pressure they are under to do so, applied by record label execs with an obvious bias to hits, since that's their job. But resist the temptation and the hits are more likely to come anyhow.

As the singer-songwriter Raye recently said, "always create with a sense of purpose, rather than the means to sell". It's tempting to make music you think people will like, or that takes on board feedback from audiences and record label staff. But making music by design doesn't make for great art. Create first for yourself and do your best work. The rest will take care of itself.

2. Obsess over your references, but meld them into something that is uniquely you

John Grant's music blends the styles of 80s synth-pop, orchestration, indie rock and folk, with strong influences from new wave, electronic music and classical arrangements – topped with his operatic baritone. That doesn't really capture it though, and indeed, Grant himself describes his sixth album, *The Art of the Lie*, by bringing in all kinds of non-musical references: "I'm trying to marry the vibe of *Blade Runner* with *Tetsuo: The Iron Man*. I want to blend Sonic Youth with *Blade Runner*, *Evil Dead* and *Halloween 3*." All of these, however, become something that sounds like nothing else except John Grant, instantly recognisable and unmistakable. It is why his debut album *Queen of Denmark* stood out from anything else being released at that time. It was a groundbreaking, genre-bending record that made such a mark on the music scene that those who have his ear have muttered that he should make another album just like it. Except he is not the kind of artist that repeats what he has already done.

In the continuous flood of new music releases, it's almost impossible to stand out. The best records contain strong themes that the creator channels in a way that is both individual and authentic. As the best authors say, write about what you know. Laura Veirs is a native of Colorado and resident of Portland, Oregon. Originally a geology major, Veirs is better known as a gifted folk-pop singer songwriter. It is no surprise that her music is steeped in nature. Her rise to fame came with 2004's *Carbon Glacier*, the first of four records themed on the elements. *Carbon Glacier* was earth, *Year of Meteors* was sky, *Saltbreakers* was sea and *July Flame* was... guess what? Fire. By the time she got around to *July Flame*, Veirs had made her first masterpiece. Let your expertise shine through – it's something that people will appreciate way beyond just being engaged or entertained.

I first came across Sea Power via their first two albums on CD. *The Decline of British Sea Power* (2003) and *Open Season* (2005) sounded like every indie band I'd ever liked, and yet like no other band at all, but I could never put my finger on why that is. The soundtrack to the film *From the Seas to the Land Beyond (2013)* made me realise that their musical influences embrace nature and the British landscape (their lyrics and themes often include birds, landscapes, and weather). Sea Power songs reference obscure historical events, military history and classic literature. They eventually dropped the 'British' from their band name as a form of protest. Their stage setups, which have included foliage and taxidermy, reflect a quirky, surreal sensibility. Over the course of two decades the band has made a batch of fine songs, solid albums, award winning soundtracks and played sold-out, highly renowned live shows.

Like John Grant and Laura Veirs, they reached beyond music to forge something that ended up sounding unique.

In a world in which there few new ideas, it's fine to beg, steal and borrow, provided you create something unique from it (if you want proof of that just think about The Rolling Stones or Coldplay). By obsessing over your references, you assimilate them. Your work stands on the shoulders of everything. As Roland Orzabal of Tears for Fears puts it: "You're altering the DNA of everything you've been listening to. Altering it, bringing it up to date, modifying it. Turning it into a higher art form." What a platform from which to launch a career in which your own music adds to a vast universe. Whatever it is, old, new, music, non-music, your job as an artist is to take those influences and make them sound like nobody else but you.

3. Work to an internal code, pact or system

Nada Surf's Matthew Caws remembers exactly when he and founding member (and bass player) Daniel Lorca solidified the code that continues to run through Nada Surf's working practices as a band to this day:

> Daniel and I walked the streets of Brooklyn in 1995 and said we would always be emotionally honest – try and speak truthfully. We don't do anything we're not comfortable with and we are okay with the chips falling the way they fall. Doing what feels good and not doing what feels bad, is important.

From day one in 1983, Manchester band James had a philosophy and pact to always take risks – whether that be creating new songs from jam sessions to walking out on stage in front of the crowd without finalising the set. As such, the band has survived the music industry changing beyond recognition since they formed, but it hasn't mattered, because they have never tried to follow musical trends or sound like any music made to a particular time. They are too busy improvising.

A musical language is essential between band members and their collaborators. Nick Cave & The Bad Seeds have something called 'the walk of shame', whereby if someone tries something out that doesn't work, they face a stony silence from the other members. While this may be the height of passive aggressiveness during a conversation with a colleague in the office, for the band it has become an essential form of honest feedback: everyone is allowed to fail and be forgiven.

Artists looking to take risks are more likely to go the distance, but to do so will mean drawing on reserves of self-belief. Something to underpin and support that self-belief is working to a code, mantra, pact or system that only the band can access, nobody else. Sometimes it's as simple as that: a few words or a simple ritual to live by and remind each other (or yourself) of why you got into a career in music in the first place.

4. Believe in your delusion

In 2002, the three remaining members of a band formed at school in Battle, Sussex pitched up to a dilapidated farmhouse an hour's drive South of Cherbourg, France. The band was called Cherry Keane and their gifted guitar player had just unexpectedly quit the band to return to Ireland. It left the band with no option but to go out to France to record their first album as a trio. The three were ambitious creatively but they were also close to giving it all up. Now placing keyboards at the centre of their sound, the band wrote and performed emotional indie rock, with just keyboards, drums and vocals adopted as their signature style. In Keane's book *Hopes and Fears: Lyrics and History* is a photograph of the page of a cheap ring bound notepad, titled "The OK Computer Test". Tim Rice-Oxley explains: "There's no way we thought we were making the next *OK Computer* but you've got to try. You ask yourself: 'how do our heroes do it'? Allowing themselves to dream, even so close to giving up, spurred Keane on to do something extraordinary. Their debut album *Hopes and Fears* became a classic, just like *OK Computer*, but with bigger hits.

There is a fantastic and surreal moment in the opening ceremony of the 2024 Paris Paralympics, in which, as President Macron exits the stage, Chilly Gonzales enters, dressed in a splendid Louis-Gabriel Nouchi cape. He cracks his knuckles, 'Bugs Bunny' style, before taking his place at the piano stool. And then plays… beautifully. You would have to be deluded to have predicted a moment like that a few years ago, but delusion, it turns out, is a key weapon in the Chilly Gonzales creative arsenal: "You must have a certain amount of delusion – to be deluded enough to believe that what you have to say deserves a platform. You have to imagine that every song you've made is worth being a hit."

In a sense, this is another way of saying that you can dare to dream. But at the same time, you don't have to dream – simply visualise your delusion and become it.

5. See line-up changes as an inevitable part of evolution

The loss of a key band member can be a punch to the stomach for any band, yet the choice remains – pick yourselves up, dust off and get on and make another record. Or don't. The blueprint for popular bands is to stay together no matter what, but that might be the very thing getting in the way and making life miserable, so cast that notion aside. It's probably better for business and for sanity to find another way forward.

Consider Mike Scott, leader of the Waterboys, who himself counts over 80 rolling band members that have come and gone. So, essentially, The Waterboys is Mike Scott? "I don't agree with that… it wouldn't be the same without the musicians. There is something about the way we play in a particular way that makes those musicians Waterboys. As much of it is as unspoken as it can be, that's for the better. It's the way we play!" And so, the Waterboys bandwagon rolls on, with Scott welcoming in new collaborators and finding himself energised by whatever they bring to the band's sound, particularly in front of the Waterboys' live audiences.

Sometimes, the loss of a member can leave a very big hole in a band. Bernard Butler was both lead guitarist and co-songwriter of the band Suede, with Brett Anderson. Butler was instrumental to Suede's glammy, dramatic 'Bowie meets the Smiths' sound. Butler left before the band had even finished their second album *Dog Man Star,* walking out due to clashes with Anderson. Butler had been such a big part of Suede, most people expected Suede to disband or fizzle out. Enter Richard Oakes, a then 17-year-old fan who had sent the band demo tapes. He got the job, and Suede's second act with Oakes, starting with third album *Coming Up*, was an unequivocal success. Suede's sound changed – more pop-oriented, concise, and accessible, it re-energised the other band members and in fact, set the band up for longevity.

But can a rock band carry on without their singer and frontperson? Manchester's Doves are one of those bands that were never in for an easy flight (pardon the pun). The band has had so many mishaps, they refer to "The curse of Doves"" recovery from an early studio fire, seeing their A&R advocates get fired from labels, an extended hiatus (during the music industry's shift to streaming), having a tour halted by COVID, and then returning to the scene at a time when the band's singer, Jimi Goodwin, was available only sporadically due to ongoing anxiety issues and recovery from addictions. This more recent development means that Doves toured their fifth album *Constellations for the Lonely* without the presence of their frontman, with twin brothers Jez and Andy Williams stepping in to share on vocal duties. As Jez told me: "We've had so many challenges put in front of us. The older you get the more you have to rise to them. It's fucking exhausting. But we are exactly where we should be." The band's three core members have some cause for optimism – the Goodwin-less tour was a sell-out – but they remain confident that at some point he'll be fit to return.

A career in music is a rolling bandwagon and every now and then, a wheel falls off. When that happens isn't a time to panic. Instead, it's time to simply take stock and maybe even change direction. But the journey can continue.

THEME 2 – MASTERING THE CRAFT

David Hockney said that "painting is harder than ideas." Making music that sounds fresh and new will get you noticed but there are no shortcuts building a career on craft. In terms of focus, we live in dangerous times, with distractions for every waking moment, but the job of an artist is to get beyond the distractions and create – a process that always takes more time than expected, sometimes years. To impress these days, bands would be advised to lock themselves away and practice for a year before even thinking about releasing a song or performing it to an audience. To stand out from the crowd you need to be way better than good (especially if you do not have a record label marketing budget behind you).

This chapter explains how successful, longevous bands have done it.

6. Get very, very good live

In the summer of 2023, I crossed London from Richmond to the Kentish Town Forum to see a band I had never seen play live before. I wasn't sure what to expect. I had gone on the basis that the Montreal trio Half Moon Run had released a fantastic album, *Salt.* Knowing the band was touring that record, I took a punt on going along. As the band took to the stage, there was an immediate sense of excitement – just a bit more than usual. It didn't take long for me to find out why.

From the opening bars of first song "You Can Let Go" to the last note of the band's 'hit' "Full Circle", the show was stunning. So much so, that some of the audience wouldn't leave the floor, somehow hoping the band might come out and do a second encore, even when we knew the curfew was up and the show was done. Two days later I was on a train north to Manchester, to catch the band again, at the city's Albert Hall. On the way into that show a fan came up to me (people do things in the North of England that you don't see in London) with fist to his heart. "This band has got me here", he said. "Well, me too" I replied, and what followed was an evening of making new friends and meeting kindred spirits. And that's music fandom at its best. Bonding through mutual love and admiration for a band that amounts to one of those 'best kept secrets'. If money and time was no object I would have followed the band across Europe. Those shows were some of the best I've ever seen.

In the modern music industry artists can blow up overnight on TikTok but struggle to sell out even small venues. That's never going to add up to a career. The only way to build that foundation is to play live. Get good at it and word of mouth will do the rest, since the appetite for live music seems to be insatiable. The second (or third) career boosts for 80s legends Tears for Fears, Duran Duran, Simple Minds and OMD have been powered by those bands' work ethic and reputation as great live acts. Most would never have made records in the first place without becoming great live performers. For solo artists the craft of playing live is even higher stakes – it's your night – the fans and everyone producing the show and performing with you are there for you. Attending a show by Suzanne Vega, Nerina Pallot, Joan As Police Woman, John Grant, is something special – shows that capture the timeless quality of the old school revue – complete with intimate banter, witty stories, comic turns and always surprising deep cuts (the choice of setlist isn't a democratic process).

Live music has bounced back from COVID to be bigger than ever, with record-breaking tours taking live music to new theatrical levels and making music concerts among the most coveted experiences. No AI will ever replace the spectacle of a real-life performance. In August 2025, cognitive scientist Lindsay A. Fleming wrote in Time Magazine: "If the past 60 years of stadium shows (and tens of thousands of years of human music-making) have taught us anything, it's that music, at its core, is about shared experience. We crave the pulse of the bass beneath our feet, the collective chant of a catchy chorus or killer bridge, the unspoken understanding between strangers who, for just one night, are part of something bigger than themselves. As technology continues to evolve and fan communities grow more interconnected, one thing is certain: the stadium concert will remain a space where we come together, not just to listen, but to belong."[9]

Whether it's a stadium or a club, honing your craft to put on a captivating live performance is what a career in music is all about. All the bands and artists that have joined me on The *Art of Longevity* podcast are formidable live acts who have put in their 10,000 hours in rehearsal rooms, festivals and out on the road. My Morning Jacket, Fink, Crowded House, Deacon Blue, Tindersticks, Death Cab For Cutie, James, Travis, David Gray, Ben Folds, Mogwai – all brilliant live.

The best gigs transport the audience to another place. We forget the world around us and live in the music for a moment.

9 'The Science of Why Humans are Obsessed with Stadium Concerts', Lindsay A. Fleming, *Time Magazine,* August 2025.

Not all gigs take us there – but the best ones do. If you can put on a performance in which people transcend into a space where they care less but dance and sing more, you will have a good shot at being around for a long, long time.

7. Make music that is 'useful'

As discussed at length in this book, *success* is highly subjective. Intrinsic success can mean more to artists than the fleeting trappings of commercial success. One recurring theme in the 'success' conversation is the simple feeling that you can make songs that are useful to people. Songs entertain and bring joy, but they also help people cope with grief, depression, break-up/divorce, illness and extraordinary experiences. Canadian indie band Metric's song "Monster Hospital" (from their second album), in what singer Emily Haines describes as "a perverse application", has helped one of the band's fans go through numerous surgical procedures despite being allergic to anaesthesia. Haines talks of Metric's music as a means of escape and sanctuary, but also as music that has a tangible, specific use – music as therapy. "I'm obsessed with the idea of usefulness. [Our music as] a salve for mental health, or even helping people in physical pain."

We are at the foothills of what music can do as clinical therapy. Music was being applied increasingly as a clinical treatment in the areas of dementia, pain relief, and a variety of mental health therapies. In 2025, Apple Music launched an initiative called Sound Therapy, described as "an innovative audio wellness collection" aimed to improve listeners' sleep, relaxation and focus. One of the benefits of social media is the direct affirmation artists can receive about just what *that* song did for someone's life, sometimes going as far as actually saving someone's life.

I often adapt a song as a theme tune. The theme tune is the song you play continuously for a period to actively help you achieve or overcome something. It is the song as 'talisman', or amulet; it can literally protect. The theme tune is right up there with the therapist, partner, parent, sibling, best friend, dog, workout or Negroni (i.e. whatever gets you through). If you keep track of your theme tunes over time, you'll end up with the most almighty powerful playlist ever – one no streaming service or algorithm could ever programme for you. Think, your very own *Desert Island Discs* but not limited to eight songs.

8. Invent a sub-genre

In 1998, Calexico's second album *The Black Light*, an album inspired by the desert of Arizona and northern Mexico, received excellent reviews and put the band firmly on the map. With their eclectic mix of cumbia, mariachi and indie-Americana, Calexico brought something new and different. Singer Joey Burns elaborates on the band's sound: "We are connected more with mariachi and cumbia than say tex-mex or tejano or norteño which has a different connection to a different tradition. For the most part we are mariachi and cumbia. I've never felt like I've mastered anything, but I'm lucky enough to play with some of those that have." Music journalist Fred Mills captured their sound perfectly with two words - 'desert noir'. What a cool subgenre to have invented. It has become part of the band's quiet legend. Despite a dearth of hits, Calexico have wandered their way through a 15-album career and still going strong.

Instrumental band Mogwai may be averse to the term 'post-rock' but it hasn't done the band any harm. Mogwai, formed in Glasgow in 1995, were not the first band to explore post-rock tropes: mood and atmosphere, quiet-loud dynamics and most importantly, crescendos. Bands like Slint, Bark Psychosis and even Talk Talk, were experimenting with post-rock elements before them. But Mogwai brought a more visceral, guitar-heavy edge to post-rock, flirting with metal, noise rock and taking crescendos to a whole new level. Their debut album *Young Team* (1997) is considered a landmark post-rock record, while the track "Like Herod", which goes from whisper-quiet to wall-of-sound fury, is one of a bunch of Mogwai songs that have become legend in the genre. Mogwai have steadily post-rocked their way to album number 12 and a sold-out world tour in 2025.

In 1998, David Gray made the album *White Ladder*, recorded with minimal production in his North London flat on a budget of £5,000. The album blended troubadour-style acoustic folk with electronic music such as drum machines, samplers, and synths. Folktronica was the label the music press attached to it at the time and *White Ladder* is widely considered to be a foundational and definitive album in the genre. The album is credited with popularizing the style and influencing a generation of artists. In a sense, Gray pioneered 'bedroom pop' two decades before it became huge on Spotify. Rex Orange County, Yellow Days, Alfie Templeman and a whole generation of bedroom pop artists owe something to Gray and *White Ladder*.

The music data website Every Noise at Once (now sadly dormant) catalogued over 1,500 genres, including hyper-niche ones like witch house, Soundcloud rap, dungeon synth and pirate metal. In 2025 alone, 'microgenres' emerging to some significance include metalstyle, dark plugg, Ivorian rock, neo-classical trap and krushclub. There may only be 12 notes in music but the permutations are endless. Inventing a subgenre isn't just a way to attract a convenient press tagline or find an instant audience – though it can help to achieve both those things. It can help you build a legacy that wins respect from your fellow musicians down the line.

9. Respect the great musicians of the past but do not try to compete with them

This is the revelation that struck Roland Orzabal of Tears for Fears as the band struggled to create a masterpiece following the runaway success of their second album *Songs from the Big Chair*. Back in the mid-80s and thrust into the pop limelight, Orzabal felt the reverence of his 60s and 70s heroes weighing heavily on his shoulders: "We were competing with the whole history of rock & roll". Buckling under that weight, Tears for Fears made one of the most tortuous and expensive albums in history. *The Seeds of Love*, an album so "opulent, expensive, puffed-up, bombastic" (Orzabal's words), they couldn't possibly follow it up. Instead, Tears for Fears imploded under the pressure. Between long gaps, the band have since come back together to make records with the belief that (even after making two of the best in pop album history) they can still create work that they consider to be as good as their best. But they now only compete with themselves, having long since stopped trying to match their heroes the way they did with *Seeds of Love*.

In Jeff Tweedy's entertaining memoir *World Within a Song*, the author, singer-songwriter and Wilco frontman says: "Taking something old and making it sound modern is nothing new." He writes of his admiration for Spanish pop sensation Rosalía: "Rosalía is forging a path for herself artistically in a way that looks positively Dylan-esque." She is indeed a great example. By filtering the ancient Spanish tradition of flamenco through postmodern pop, driven by beats and ultra-modern production, Rosalía has found a fresh way to embellish her powerful songs. In 2025 Rosalía went further, creating the album *Lux*, an ambitious, genre-defying album 'in four movements', this time fusing classical and opera music with contemporary pop, electronic and hip-hop – inspired not just by classical musicians but the saints. Rosalía has found a divine path to longevity and legend!

New York-based indie band The Walkmen formed in 2000 following the breakup of two separate bands: Jonathan Fire*Eater and The Recoys, who had been heavily associated with post-punk and garage rock. In turn, those bands were influenced by the emergent scene of American alternative indie bands in the 80s, many of which could easily be forgotten, except for being immortalised in the book *Our Band Could Be Your Life: Scenes from the American Indie Underground, 1981–1991* by Michael Azzerad. The band Minutemen were a particular inspiration to The Walkmen, but the band's ethos was to respect the past but not try to repeat it. Minutemen were essentially pioneers of unclassifiable, post-genre rock, something carried forward into the 2000s by the Walkmen, who made six albums leading up to the highly accomplished 2012 album *Heaven*, after which the band went on a decade-long hiatus.

The music industry is set up to drop musicians into a competition, by squeezing songs into playlists and charts, handing out nominations and awards and allocating bands onto hierarchic festival slots. It's enough to give musicians a complicated relationship with competition. Some creative rivalries have worked wonders in pushing artists to reach new limits, yet the best bands compete with themselves whilst being aware of those whose shoulders they stand on.

10. Before you make your first album, make sure you have written two – hold something back

Foster the People's second album *Supermodel* was produced by superstar hitmaker Paul Epworth and given top priority by major label Columbia Records, looking to capitalise on the unexpected success of the 2011 debut *Torches*, with its phenomenal hit "Pumped Up Kicks". But the album was a hot mess of styles that just wouldn't gel. The band has kept going but have struggled to make their mark in the wake of their debut, a shame, as their fourth album *Paradise State of Mind* achieves what they were looking for back in 2014.

After debut success on a major label, so many bands have gotten bogged down. For a classic 'sophomore slump' story, take the UK hard rock band the Darkness. After the success of debut album *Permission to Land*, the band was snapped up by a major label (Atlantic) and thrust into the music industry hype machine. Their second album *One Way Ticket to Hell... and Back* featured mellotrons, sitars, orchestras, bagpipes, everything except the kitchen sink. Let's just say it lacked the urgency of their debut. After the record flopped, the Darkness almost fell apart and didn't make another album for seven years. It's been good to see their recent renaissance.

The 'difficult second album' remains a pivotal moment for most artists. It is a key bridge to potential long-term success. Most examples of failed sophomore records either try too hard to repeat a successful debut or are a collection of rushed out songs to capitalise on initial momentum. It may seem like an advantage – the idea of building on early acclaim and attention, but songs can't be made to order, and artists often find the pressure of the follow up paralysing. Glasgow band Belle and Sebastian found a neat solution to the difficult second album. By the time the band's precocious debut *Tigermilk* was released in 1996, singer and songwriter Stuart Murdoch already had another album written. Many believe that second album, *If You're Feeling Sinister*, to be their best.

It's easy to forget just how massive Scottish band Travis got to be with their second and third albums, *The Man Who* (1999) and *The Invisible Band* (2001). They sold millions of albums and were all over UK radio. But in Fran Healy, the band has a songwriter whose abundance has been a key source of quality material. But Healy doesn't write songs to order. In his words, he is a "song diviner not a song designer". That means that, when inspiration strikes, he'll write, saving ideas and whole songs in the bank for now or later, including albums three or four. As Healy says,

> If you're 23 when you make your first album, you've been working on it for 23 years. The hardest thing is when you get to your third album and you only have a year to make it. You need to hold songs back for that, which we had with *Writing to Reach You*.

If you keep writing good songs, there's always a place to store them for later. A way to mitigate the dreaded difficult second album is to have enough songs in the bag for two albums before your debut comes out. I have a theory that the difficult second album is now really the fourth. This is partly because artists no longer sign multiple album deals but tend to make records independently, so they can keep going without being tied to one record label. And partly because younger fans don't engage with albums until they have followed a band for many years. In short, artists and bands need to make albums of consistently high quality now, they cannot afford to make weak or rushed albums. It means storing up a bank of good songs and always holding something back for the future.

11. Make your songs a bit weird

There are few hitmakers as masterful as Nile Rodgers (his beat-up 1959 Fender Stratocaster is even nicknamed 'The Hitmaker', estimated to have played a role in songs worth over $2 billion). When Rodgers took control of David Bowie's early folk rendition of "Let's Dance" and turned it into Bowie's biggest commercial success, the creative result was one of the best singles of the 80s. But the song was, in Rodgers' own words, *weird*. Everyone involved knew that "Let's Dance" was special, but it sounded like no other song ever to reach the top of the charts. Despite the songwriting-by-numbers culture in the streaming era, it's worth remembering that audiences are people, and people can be a bit weird.

The Wombats have the close-knit quality of a pop three-piece, a collaborative unit of multi-instrumentalists, all trained in music and sound production at Liverpool's LIPA. They have ridden a wave of 'pop as the new indie', adjusting their sound to be something beyond their early post-punk/grunge guitars of the early 2000s. At the core of their success are their songs – catchy, bouncy, poppy earworms – at least a dozen of which have topped 100 million streams. The band, once written off by the UK music press as "indie landfill", have become a huge, sustained success. However, pulling the rug from under their catchy pop songs is also part of the Wombats' songcraft. Clever use of bridges or sudden shifts in tone can make the difference between a predictable pop song and something a bit weirder but more memorable. The Wombats have become adept at constructing the modern pop song with a twist.

Hitmaking has been part of pop's formula since the music industry began. Is there anything more cynical than those anodyne pop ballads written for daytime radio? But formulaic pop songs now have some serious competition. AI can be trained mercilessly on hits. The more formulaic the hit, the quicker AI will make perfect copies that will flood onto playlists and take up space on the charts once occupied by real musicians. To protect yourself from AI substitutes, lean into your weirdness. It worked for the Beatles, Bowie and Björk.

12. Welcome in those little details that might change your destiny aka trust your studio team

Back in 1992, the Barenaked Ladies' song "One Week" finally broke the band in the USA and brought them international fame. Although Ed Robertson had written the song and taken lead vocals duty (including that infamous rap) Ed thought the record label's suggestion to make "One Week" the lead single for their new album was a joke. But it wasn't the rap causing the problem, it was the drums. The record's producer Susan Rogers suggested the drum loop "wasn't very cool". The band changed the drums, a tweak which transformed the song, and, in effect, the band's entire future.

In 1990, Los Lobos hauled themselves into a downtown LA studio with six new songs and teamed up with producer Mitchell Froom together with engineer Tchad Blake. Steve Berlin reflects on those sessions: "Nothing could sound normal, it had to be noisy, turned upside down. Tchad could even take the mistakes and turn them into something that sounded genius." That project turned into Los Lobos' masterpiece album *Kiko*. It's well known that some of our favourite records contain human errors and studio mistakes and other imperfections that were left on the record only to improve it in the end. Those imperfections on classic pop records couldn't be easily fixed with computer software or studio sounds. Perhaps that's why manufactured or AI pop songs don't stand the test of time.

While Fink is not a band to bend to the whims of the record industry (band leader Fin Greenall told me "I've never tried to write a hit"), on 2014's *Hard Believer* album, along came the song "Looking Too Closely". An exercise in restraint, it doesn't rely on a big chorus or any kind of hook, yet Greenall still felt like it was a more commercial song than the band usually creates, so much so that his first instinct was to throw it out: "I wanted to cut it from the album, but my manager said they would walk away if I did." Now that is good management. The song was initially given away as a free download, but 150 million streams later, Fink has a genuine streaming hit – something that gave the band the freedom to do whatever they wanted from that point on.

Those small suggestions, accidents and tweaks can turn out to be pivotal, so open your ears to those suggestions. It might be your manager or record label, or a collaborator, partner or friend, but sometimes the smallest amount of input can blow up to career-defining significance. Producers and engineers really can make careers. Your inner circle are the people that really matter most. Listen closely to what they say to you.

13. Create in a vacuum but have an appreciation of how the market works

It is clear when artists have made music for the market, and sometimes it works. But the world's best-selling albums were created in a vacuum. As David Bowie once said "Never play to the gallery. I think it's terribly dangerous for an artist to fulfil other people's expectations, I think they generally produce their worst work when they do that." Yet it also helps for artists to *know* their market, so that they can be aware of the potential of what they have created. Once you have finished the record, it helps to be obliging and understanding when it comes to the commercial requirements of a label, whose job it is to sell it. Marketing and promoting a record are best done as a meeting of minds, not a fight over what should be the single or who the target audience is. With hindsight, many legacy artists wish they had paid more attention to music marketing. They wish they had shown more patience and participation in the process, even if they found the idea difficult at the time.

For this example, we'll return for the last time to our longevity guru Chilly Gonzales. Gonzales is a classically-trained musician who found success in the growing genre of neoclassical piano music. He is equal parts a classical composer, rapper, performance artist, producer, muse, entertainer and avant-garde 'artiste'. However, once he has completed a creative project – whatever it is – he prepares to flip from the mindset of the artist to the role of marketer. He's ready to do what it takes in promoting his music, with no complaints about jumping on the treadmill. Instead, he gets creative about it. Among other publicity stunts, he has proclaimed himself "President of the Berlin Underground" and referred to himself, tongue firmly in cheek (or is it?), as a musical genius, or, more recently embodying his "Gonzo" persona, appearing on stage in a dressing gown – a satirical take on artistic ego but at the same time a marketing strategy that earns his music an unfair competitive edge when it comes to press coverage and word-of-mouth publicity. It would not surprise me at all if at some stage, "a sensational new AI artist" turns out to be… Gonzales. His method is to "flip a switch inside your head" and enjoy the process of marketing your creation.

Today's music business is more collaborative, with both artists and labels required to play major roles in marketing, preferably with a joined-up strategy. Enjoy the process for what it is: a sales pitch for the best product in the world – your music.

THEME 3 – MANAGING EXPECTATIONS

An artistic career is a tough choice and a hard road. It's good to want an audience. It's natural to seek affirmation, even admiration. And the idea that you can create what you love and make a living from it, even become *famous* for it, is a dream worth coveting. But what if you make a song and nobody gets to hear it? All artists go through the struggle phase and may find the creative path intolerably hard. But since the struggle is a universal concept all artists go through, is there a way to accept it and enjoy it?

14. 'Enjoy' the struggle

The National are a band whose ascendancy has been a steady rise to recognition as one of the best bands in the world, certainly one quoted by many musicians and fans as being their favourite 'alternative' band. The National are an exception to the boom and bust of Brett Anderson's 'Stations of the Cross' career curve. Their first two albums were released on their own small label, and the following two, *Alligator* and *Boxer*, were released on the indie label Beggars Banquet, noticed by critics but not reaching the album charts. The fourth LP *High Violet* was a breakthrough, receiving critical acclaim and hitting the top 10 in the UK, USA and many other countries around the world. After 10 years of struggling to get noticed, *High Violet* set the National on a course for the best possible version of band superstardom – a steady climb to arena shows, major festival headline slots and increasing record sales with each release. The members of the band have branched out into highly successful solo and collaborative projects, with the band's creative community drawing in Taylor Swift, Phoebe Bridgers, Booker T. Jones and Justin Vernon. If a band could write the manual for longevity, I would nominate the National. Matt Berninger, the band's enigmatic and cerebral frontman (and unlikely rock star), is grateful for the band's trajectory, including the early years of struggle:

> We were ignored for the first couple of records, nobody paid attention to us until *Alligator* and *Boxer*. Those records were hard fought, but by then, we had four records and so you couldn't hold us down. Then Annie Clark (St. Vincent) and Sufjan Stephens started helping us and we grew this community in Brooklyn that became a really healthy thing for all of us.

David Gray's first three albums, released between 1993 and 1996, made Gray known in folk-rock circles, but failed in terms of commercial sales (despite his third being ironically titled *Sell, Sell, Sell*). He was signed and dropped by labels, twice. Then came *White Ladder*. It was one of those CDs *everybody* had. It came at the end of the CD era, one of the last albums that achieved cultural ubiquity. To get to *White Ladder*, Gray went through a necessary process. Indeed, after the phenomenal success of *White Ladder* wore off, he became acutely aware that he would go through a similar process of 'post-fame' adjustment all over again. When I interviewed

Gray on *The Art of Longevity* he articulated this perfectly: "Once you get attention and then lose it, how do you get it back? It's a question I've been puzzling over for a long time." He gradually came to see it as simply another form of struggle. Even though he was 'famous' and more comfortable financially, the struggle became the continual challenge for both creative satisfaction and recognition.

In today's music business, there is no destination named 'success'. If you hit 10 million streams with your first EP, you must then do it again, and then work out how to be great live, and then how to make money. You are likely to work with multiple labels, perhaps several different managers. It may *always* feel like a struggle, even when everyone else tells you that you are succeeding. See the struggle as a natural part of the process.

15. Define your own version of success

On measuring the success of a new album (2025 release *Dreams on Toast*), Justin Hawkins, frontman of the British rock band the Darkness, told *The Creative Independent*:

> The goal posts will have moved four or five times during the process of making the record. You won't know what success looks like. You don't know how to quantify what the metrics are to tell you whether you've done a good job or not. You don't know. People don't buy records anymore, but you've got streaming, and who cares about streaming? People my age don't. Then you've got to think about social media and interviews and stuff like that. It's like the real work starts when you finish recording.

The music industry no longer has one central idea of success. The charts mean less than they used to, awards are a flash in the pan and radio play has no tangible impact on record sales (which no longer exist). If it seems like social media metrics and playlists are the way to build success, that can be strangely discombobulating from the actual process of releasing records. The modern music industry is a disorientating place in which attribution and validation can be strangely hard to find. Manchester indie pop band Everything Everything has released seven albums, six of which have reached the UK top 10. Frontman Jonathan Higgs told me that the band sometimes feels as if they never have a handle on whether they are doing well:

> We have business meetings where we talk about a sort of grand strategy. And the main topic of conversation is basically like, how are we doing as a band? We don't really know. We just got a top 10 album, but we feel like we're invisible. Our Spotify listeners are doing great. But we were not being played on the radio. Like, where are we? Who are we? It's difficult to tell.

It's a common curse and persistent dull migraine for many bands. Artists are creatively ambitious. They seek a sense of forward momentum that encapsulates creative progression, the respect of peers, a growing fan base and, finally, making enough money. But success is in the eye of the beholder. In my previous role with the music insight agency MIDiA Research, I wrote a report for the distribution company Amuse, based on artist interviews.[10] That report boiled down success to some combination of the following factors:

---

10 "Sustainability from Chaos: How today's artists find sustainable success in a turbulent music industry', M. Mulligan, K. Jopling, H. Kahlert et al., MIDiA Research.

- *Sustainability* – to be able to make a living and ultimately give up the day job
- *Recognition* – from peers in a scene and from audience numbers, but also from audience feedback
- *Progression* – to improve as an artist from the perspective of creation, performance and recognition
- *Longevity* – to have a career that will last, with creative twists and turns that will bring some fans along and win over new ones, while losing others
- *Legacy* – to build a catalogue of work that has a chance to be evergreen, recurring, and recognised over time

This is a solid summary of what success really means. Keeping this list in mind will keep you sane in a music industry awash with buzz metrics, viral hits and chart spikes. If you get to make a record and then make another – and make music for a living – you are, by any meaningful measure, a success.

16. Earn the right to say no, and be prepared to fight for what you want

Matt Hales is an English singer, songwriter, musician and record producer who has been performing professionally under the name Aqualung since the early 2000s. Aqualung had a big breakthrough in the UK with the song "Strange & Beautiful (I'll Put a Spell on You)", which was featured on a television advertisement for the new Volkswagen Beetle during the summer of 2002 and went on to become a top 10 hit. Hales couldn't repeat the trick. Instead, he went on to make his name and build his career in the USA, much of it through hard, steady touring – the opposite of the "instant success" he experienced in the UK. Aqualung bucked the trend for under-achieving British acts in America during the noughties, selling a hundred thousand albums, receiving Grammy nominations and appearing on Jay Leno's Tonight Show. Matt Hales became what he calls "inadvertently cool". How did that happen? "I tried compromising at one stage, by writing hits and giving the A&R guy what he wanted, but it made me unhappy. So I made the quietest music I could, my *Idagio*, my own quiet *Pet Sounds*. That turned out to be successful anyway!"

Once he turned away from trying to make another hit, Hales established a parallel music career by becoming a successful, sought-after writer-producer, collaborating with Lianne La Havas (he produced her superb debut album), Bat for Lashes, Tom Chaplin, Mika, Paloma Faith, Disclosure and most recently pop star Olivia Dean.

> I'm very lucky a few things have worked out. You could say I'm a spoilt bastard, because I can afford to be philosophical [about success] because I get paid. Artists are so beset by statistics these days it's easy to feel sorry for them. But you can make uncompromising music that you love and also have it succeed. You don't always have to make a pact with the devil or pimp yourself out.

Hales has released no less than seven albums as Aqualung – a 'one-hit wonder' that achieved longevity, including success in America, becoming a favourite of TV music supervisors, a go-to writer-producer for rising stars and, all the time, a steadily developing musician and performer. His advice to the many young musicians he now works with is be prepared to "fight for it, like having a little chick that you need to keep alive. Why would you ever think it might be easy!"

Tears for Fears are a truly iconic British pop duo that holds the highest accolade in songwriting – an Ivor Novello award for Outstanding Song Collection. For the band's 2022 album *The Tipping Point*, Roland Orzabal and Curt Smith were locked in a songwriting camp for over a year, with an elite group of hitmaker writers and producers in (a fruitless) search for hit tunes. Eventually, Orzabal and Smith abandoned the project altogether. Instead, they started from scratch as a duo – the way they wrote songs 40 years ago for the *The Hurting*. The band and their new label were understandably cautious about the impact of a new album after a long absence. In 2022, songwriting camps and multiple songwriters had become the norm for artists seeking hits. But when it came down to it, the two (this is Tears for Fears after all) needed no outside help.

As the music industry heads further towards new levels of technologisation and commodification, it is heartening to know that some things never really change. Despite the best efforts of AI, audio software and large teams of songwriters, the very best songs are still created in the old way. The best music is the sum of the artists' choices. Ultimately as listeners, we are embracing that idea and enjoying the fruits of their singular vision. In making those choices, be ready to turn down what doesn't feel right, even if those around you think it is.

17. Have the confidence to disrupt yourself before the industry disrupts you

After Norah Jones' 4th album *The Fall* in 2009 proved to be a departure from her well-known blend of blues-jazz-country-pop, Norah Jones recalls receiving a fan letter:

> After I made The Fall, I received the sweetest letter from a fan in Argentina, but it was also criticising me as well. It said 'I'm a really big fan but would you please go back to singing the ballads, because you do that better and I really need that from you'. It was a sweet letter but I decided then, you are never going to please everyone.

Selling over 30 million copies worldwide, Jones' colossal debut *Come Away with Me* restored faith among record labels that they could still have massive hit albums, even as Napster and file-sharing was tearing the recording industry apart. It was one of the most successful jazz/pop crossover albums ever, propelling Jones into a long career as a major artist, even if the record became something of an albatross given her desire to experiment and transcend music genres. Was *The Fall* a deliberate rebellion against the mould? Yes and no seems to be the answer. Jones was always a creator without boundaries, it was simply her massive early following (including the author of that fan letter) that placed certain expectations on her music. Her next album was the hugely impressive and experimental *Little Broken Hearts* (2012, with Danger Mouse). After that record, her friend, mentor and boss Bruce Lundval, CEO of Blue Note, thought things had gone too far. He told Jones over lunch "I've got to be honest with you I didn't really like this record at first. It's not your thing." That lunch may have had more impact than the fan letter, but only up to a point. The 2016 album *Day Breaks* brought back the jazz, but the experimental elements from working with Danger Mouse had rubbed off, giving Norah's work an edge – something to make the more 'indie' listener prick up their ears. It means her audience has more substance than her initial burst of popularity.

The Lumineers' song "Plasticine" gives a glimpse of the pressures placed on the artist to conform to music industry formulas. It's one of a thousand songs that rail against the ways of the music business, that moulds and shapes artists to become something they don't want to become. The Lumineers first blew up with a ragtag debut album that was a mess of genres. They had success (over two billion streams) with a simple guitar-based folk song called "Ho Hey" and their live shows went down a storm. But in Wesley Schultz's words, the Lumineers at that time were: "compassless, there was no rudder to it. We were middle school, wearing sweater-vests. But we weren't stuck either." They submitted a follow-up album, *Cleopatra*, to their label without anyone hearing it. And the lead single (the title track) was a simple ballad with no guitar. Instead, its centre was Jeremiah Fraites' deeply uncool, twinkly piano motif. But that lead single also went huge. *Cleopatra* was produced with Simon Felice, highly respected but way off the hitmaker radar. The only songwriters were Schultz and Fraites. "The secret of longevity for us, is we get to make our records and nobody else hears it until it's done. And that's it."

The Lumineers' booking agent Alex Bruford told them "Everybody wants Radiohead's career" and it's a truism. Radiohead exemplifies the artist who doesn't compromise creatively, the artist who can take a 180-degree turn and make it work in their favour, dignity intact. A new generation of bands coming up in today's frantic music business want a career like the Lumineers. Many musicians are intuitive enough to know what record label execs do not; that staying in your lane will send you quickly down a cul-de-sac.

18. Keep in mind that your best work is ahead of you

No artist wants to be their own echo. David Hepworth's book *Hope I Get Old Before I Die*, examines the dilemma new artists face with making new material after their big hit records. Hepworth points out that for some artists, the peak of their success can be something of an albatross:

> Most artists prefer to think the reason they're there is to write and record new songs – songs which, they always say in interviews, are among the best things they have ever done. That may or may not be the case… it is very unusual for an artist to go on selling records beyond their second decade.[11]

One of the challenges of staying relevant is a kind of creative reconciliation between the artist's most popular works (their 'old stuff') and their most recent project. Hepworth's idea sounds true, but I doubt it still applies to the modern era of music. I've never known a time like it for 'old bands' making great new music – and having their new songs accepted by their fan base. I've seen a few live shows in which artists announce new songs almost apologetically. But the attitudes of audiences have changed and it's no longer necessary.

One of those artists who can be self-deprecating about new material is Nerina Pallot. After her second album *Fires*, Nerina Pallot was suddenly hot property on the music scene circa 2007. Never quite comfortable with that, she attempted to head in a more edgy direction with her third album *The*

---

11 *Hope I Get Old Before I Die: Why Rock Stars Never Retire*, David Hepworth. Penguin Randon House.

Graduate (2009). But it was an uneven record that failed to build on the momentum of *Fires*. It turned out for the better in the long run. Pallot regrouped to make a more consistent and accomplished record (*Year of the Wolf*) in 2011. It became a foundation for what she continues to do – make finely-crafted records of grown-up pop music. Some eight albums into her career, it feels like her albums are still getting better.

When David Gray joined me on *The Art of Longevity* podcast, I was so taken with his new album *Dear Life* (released January 2025) that it seemed churlish to dwell on his earlier career success with the ubiquitous *White Ladder*. Gray told me:

> I'm always all in with the new stuff. If I wasn't I would just retire. It's always a moment of total commitment. I like the danger of writing and recording. There is gold in them there hills and you have got to go and find it. I feel like these songs are strong enough to go shoulder to shoulder with the big songs.

Bringing back Brett Anderson's words from earlier: "As soon as you think you've done your best work, it's game over." Many of the artists featured on *The Art of Longevity* have made superb recent albums, including Travis, Tindersticks, Mogwai, Rickie Lee Jones, Idlewild, Morcheeba, The Charlatans, Crowded House, My Morning Jacket, and Norah Jones. And indeed, Suede, whose one-two punch of *Autofiction* (2023) and then *Antidepressants* (2025) counts among their best work. Bands from as far back as the 80s are still making superb albums now, notably Depeche Mode, OMD, Duran Duran and even after long absences, the Cure and Pulp.

In a recent *Guardian* review for Bryan Ferry's new album *Loose Talk* (with artist Amelia Barratt), Alexis Petredis writes: "There comes a point in every August artist's career where they're forced to make an accommodation with their own past, a tacit acknowledgment that anything new they release exists in the shadow of their own back catalogue." Even if that is true, it's in the job description for artists to fight against this notion and prove the critics wrong.

19. Have other pursuits outside of your main music vehicle

Corey Taylor is probably best known as Slipknot #9 (lead vocals) but before he joined Slipknot, Taylor already had another established hard rock band, Stone Sour. Taylor has released two solo albums. He is also a *New York Times* bestselling author and has written four books, in addition to several comic book projects. He has taken acting roles and is an outspoken advocate for mental health awareness, particularly among youth and up-and-coming music artists. This multiple persona artist is a blueprint for music creators in this day and age. After all, to put all your creative eggs in one basket is risky in today's ultra-competitive music market. Not a problem for Corey Taylor. He has too many ideas and too much restless energy to fit into just one band, even if it is one of the world's biggest and most successful metal bands. So how does he do it?

> I'm able to prioritise and focus to get the best out of me creatively. My appetite for art and creating is insatiable though – I've got so many things I want to do, it keeps me sane and grounded. I'm hyper-focused but I do things bit by bit. But maybe I'm also just a psycho.

It used to be that 'solo projects' for members of bands were considered equivalent to cheating in a marriage. But monogamy (I'm still talking about bands here) can lead to boredom and burnout. That's what happened to the Walkmen. The band is made up of five Washington DC natives: Hamilton Leithauser, Paul Maroon, Matt Barrick, Walter Martin and Peter Bauer. None of them did solo projects but dedicated themselves to the band they had formed together as young friends in their early 20s. As Hamilton Leithauser described it:

> We were caught in this marriage we couldn't get out of. It's exhausting physically and mentally - in the long run. After you've done a bunch of records you think 'do I really wanna do another rock & roll record, no I don't think I do', then it becomes about what you really want to do next.

It led to a 10-year hiatus for the Walkmen, a period that finally allowed the band members some precious time to explore their own creative pastures. As they return to the music scene, tentatively, the five members take a different outlook to what it is to be in a band, i.e. not a be-all-and-end-all situation. Long-standing rock bands like the National, Radiohead and Wilco boast members with a multitude of solo work, side-projects, successful writer-producer collaborations and other artistic endeavours, and the more work they take on the longer the core bands continue to thrive, even with longer gaps between albums and tours. Those other projects bring another dimension to their careers and provide much needed space, time and oxygen.

Much is made about the ageing of the fan. Fans associate bands with the era in which they first connected, and so bands end up stuck in a kind of time capsule. Meanwhile, they also have lives to get on with *outside* the all-consuming music business. Between the intensity of writing and recording and the hard graft of touring, the obsessive nature of music makes work-life balance extremely difficult, virtually impossible. Ignore the advice from tech bros and marketing managers about being an 'always on' creator, leave that to social media content creators.

For decades, the music industry has ignored notions such as motherhood, parental leave, health & wellness, time off or any of the other expected norms of the workplace. It makes for a specific set of challenges for artists when it comes down to living a 'normal life'. But longevity isn't about fear of being forgotten. If the fan base needs to wait a while, then let them wait. It just builds the excitement for your return.

20. Take your time

The actor Tony Curtis famously once said "My longevity is down to timing." In this day & age, when instant gratification drives so much music 'consumption', taking the time to create songs of beauty and meaning isn't going to get any easier. But doing just that will continue to be what sets you apart. Artists are told they need to be "on 24/7". They need to be influencers, they need to release more music, they need to release more *content*. They need to work harder. It's no secret that record labels want to sign artists with a social media following, so they don't have to do the work to develop or market them. Labels are looking for low risk shortcuts to making more money – and that means signing artists who have already become successful on some level.

A career is built song by song, gig by gig and fan by fan. Success in music is mostly about perseverance. That great song, that classic album, that appointment with success – can come at any time, but you don't get to decide the timings (Tony Curtis was only joking) and you don't control the forces which align all the stars. The truth is, there is no point racing to the front of an endless surge of music – you'll just get crushed.

Afterword #1 – Coming back from a lost world

When the Cure released their first album in 17 years, *Songs of a Lost World*, singer and pop music icon Robert Smith returned to promotional duties (even rock royalty must do promo). Smith reluctantly gave a few short interviews. In one of these, he told BBC Radio 6 Music, "It's nice how attention has returned to us". That short statement contains a multitude – it contains this book! Robert Smith was right, attention had returned to the Cure. But why, how? For a few years leading up to the *Songs of a Lost World* the Cure slowly re-surfaced after many quiet years.

The Cure has nearly 20 million monthly listeners on Spotify these days (although they are yet to reach The Billions Club, it's only a matter of time). But if you go back a few years – to June 2018, the band was at five million monthly listeners. Back then, big hits like "Boys Don't Cry" and "Friday I'm in Love" were still played on the radio, but not much else was happening around the band. Since then, there has been a wave of nostalgia for 1980s/90s alternative rock & pop. The Cure's 2018 *Mixed Up* reissue got the band's more alternative songs back on to playlists, and their Glastonbury 2019 headline slot boosted wider interest (even to the extent that Smith's signature Schecter guitars saw a spike in sales). By June 2020, the Cure's monthly listeners on Spotify had doubled to ten million, so to Smith's point, something was beginning to happen. The pandemic-era streaming surges helped legacy acts, and the Cure was a part of that, too. Then, as TikTok took off, their classic album *Disintegration* (1989) became a cult favourite. TikTok has fuelled a resurgence of interest in goth, post-punk, and 80s alternative music, and so, the Cure eventually joined the platform in October 2023.

Earlier, in 2022, the Cure embarked on a massive world tour to begin to preview *Songs of a Lost World*. When finally released a few years later, the album created a whole new buzz about the Cure, reaching number one in the UK (and number four in the USA) – their highest chart positions since the 80s. The Cure's management and label worked meticulously, capitalising on the Cure's goodwill with the music media and the band's phenomenal influence on today's music scene. Despite the Cure's seemingly long 'absence', it didn't take much for the band to be welcomed back. Then again, it didn't all happen by chance.

Robert Smith didn't say all that, because pop icons don't have to. "It's nice how attention has returned to us" will do just fine!

Afterword # 2 – Who is next for rock legend?

It has been fantastic to see the Cure return to the modern music scene with such impact. But in music, there is nothing better than a new band in the ascendant – an unstoppable upward trajectory. New artists and bands are always a cause for excitement and celebration for both the music industry and fans alike. What is it about our obsession with the new? We hope that a new artist or band can become a legend of tomorrow. We want an artist to progress in depth and breadth – opening new creative worlds for us with a series of brilliant albums. We want them to create a body of work that rivals the legends we love. None of this can happen without a support system that helps discover, develop and sustain music talent. I feel like this is especially true in the rock world. Perhaps because we put 'classic rock' on a pedestal – the four- or five-piece band represents the perfect rock & roll dream. I've no doubt that Oasis' phenomenal early success was down to their youth, bravado and great songs but also that we are always ready to welcome a great new rock & roll band, because there isn't anything much better. And yet rock bands on that level are so rare. Streaming hasn't been kind to rock. No wonder Oasis enjoyed the most successful comeback tour ever – there are hardly any other rock bands around to steal their limelight, even two decades after they left the scene. Not only do the economics of the music business no longer work in bands' favour, but streaming has been such a boost to other types of music – hip hop, rap, pop, Latin music and more recently country, that rock has been crowded out, and subsequently given the "Cinderella" treatment by many record labels.

We want new bands to succeed, but they very rarely do. When a new band comes along – from Wet Leg to The Last Dinner Party – everyone in the music business is so excited that they are thrown headlong into the industry hype cycle, just as rock bands ever were. This doesn't set them up for long term success. The later sections of a band's career journey are made harder by the 'stratospheric rise to the top', because in today's music business, nobody really knows where 'the top' is.

Here is a situation analysis for five of those bands with the potential to become legends. I've picked out British and Irish bands here, only because these are close to home for me, and in the particularly British tradition of exporting rock bands to the rest of the world. Curiously, that hasn't yet happened for all these bands – yet. But based on everything I've learned putting together this book, I'm betting on these bands to go the distance…

Fontaines D.C.

The Dublin (as in D.C.) band consists of Grian Chatten (vocals), Conor Curley (guitar), Conor Deegan III (bass), Tom Coll (drums) and Carlos O'Connell (guitar). I heard Fontaines described as "the best band in the world" three times in the space of a week by people on the radio, such was the band's ascendancy curve in 2024-25. The band's fourth album *Romance* took them to "the next level" (i.e. closer to 'the top'). Frontman and lyricist Grian Chatten has a way with words and a suitably nonchalant stage presence. Live, the band is exciting, if still developing their stagecraft for bigger venues and festival headline slots. If anything, post *Romance* will require Fontaines to hold it down and stay grounded, as there is an obvious danger of them becoming over-hyped. If longevous bands have their best work ahead of them, legend beckons for Fontaines D.C. Their success has already paved a way for a crop of new Irish alternative/guitar bands, including New Dad, Gurriers, Sprints and the Murder Capital, so in some ways a legacy exists already. For a band who has emphasised roots so much, including in their name, where next?

Wolf Alice

Wolf Alice formed in London in 2010 as a duo but Singer Ellie Rowsell and guitarist Joff Oddie then bolstered the band to a classic four piece, adding bassist Theo Ellis and drummer Joel Amey. As Chrissie Hynde says: "is there anything better than a four-piece rock & roll band?" The answer isn't lost on Wolf Alice. It's clear the band are enjoying their roller-coaster ride (upwards) towards bigger stages and are working extremely hard at it. The stakes have been raised for Wolf Alice – a decision they've made for themselves, 'switching up' from an indie (Dirty Hit) to a major label, Columbia Records for their fourth album *The Clearing*. Here is what I write about *The Clearing* in the book *Body of Work*: "The band can't make a bad song, and these 11 tracks hang together in the manner of a late-70s classic. I'm plumping for this album to endure and make its mark for one of Britain's best rock prospects".

The Clearing sets the band up very well for bigger tours and festival headline slots, with Emily Eavis no doubt having their phone number at the ready for the big call up (if Glastonbury still wants rock bands as headliners). Like Fontaines D.C., Wolf Alice has yet to break the US, probably top-of-mind for Columbia Records. Next level success and longevity seem almost assured, but does the band want even more than that?

The 1975

Many would argue the 1975 have already reached legend status and they are the 'biggest' band on this list. Headlining the Pyramid Stage at Glastonbury in 2025 was a significant test for a relatively young band in a global music scene dominated by solo artists (at the superstar level). Having had all five of their albums reach number one in the UK, the Manchester band are the only ones on this list to have cracked the US market, hence their enormous following on streaming platforms. Remarkably, the band has demonstrated how to be "an album band" in the song-dominated streaming age – they have only had minor chart hits (even if those songs go on to be massive streamers). For music fans of a certain age, the 1975 are a throwback to the height of 80s pop and yet Matty Healy is a frontman and lyricist (overarching themes are digital life, mental health, and modern romance) very much occupied with the tribulations of the modern era. The band are impressive live performers. Reviewing their highly theatrical tour for the band's fifth album *Being Funny in a Foreign Language*, the writer Dorian Lynskey reported (in the *Guardian*) "So begins a wonderfully strange, and estranging, experiment in what arena rock can be."

The 1975 is a rare entity in the current music landscape – a British band with international success. But, is the band already legend? The 1975 are divisive – even across generations of music fans – holding them off from 'mainstream success' in the way achieved by previous era bands such as Coldplay, U2 or even Radiohead. Can the 1975 make an album that transcends their 'millennial pop' reputation and win over the doubters? It probably doesn't matter to them one bit, but in many ways, it matters to the British music industry, which cannot afford to lose the knack for producing rock bands that become huge cultural exports. If only the band would take themselves more seriously… but would that backfire, creatively?

Sam Fender

I'm adding Fender to the list even though he is, of course, technically, a solo artist. However, Fender has a core band of loyal sidemen – his close mates. Even if they don't ever become household names, they are to Sam what the E Street Band is to Bruce Springsteen, with whom he is of course, compared. Is he worthy? The music industry must always make such comparisons but in this case, who would argue? He is the Springsteen of South Shields, The North of England, even the whole of Britain. Fender has already won over Glastonbury (calling card for future headline slot duly left on the Eavis desk) and even receives advice from Sting. Sam Fender is a superstar, although there is a question mark over whether he wants to be. That will have his major label reps in regular night sweats.

Three (UK number one) albums in, the expectations are for a fourth record that qualifies as a masterpiece, but preferably with another theme along the lines of bona fide hit "Seventeen Going Under" or early classic "Dead Boys". His third album *People Watching* was a more polished and mainstream production (it won the 2025 Mercury Music Prize) but as such, lacked anthems. Even if breaking the USA shouldn't be a priority or a necessity, it feels like no other artist is rendering rock & roll quite like Sam Fender, stepping into territory forever occupied by American artists. Sam Fender seems to have all the required elements: anthemic songs, real deal working-class roots, fantastic stage presence, a great band and classic album credentials. He is yet another potentially great artist under the wing of a major label (did you think major labels were just TikTok addicts?). Perhaps the more telling question is whether the modern music industry can accommodate and nurture such a talent into global stardom. And is he up for it?

Nothing but Thieves

Formed in 2012 in Southend-on-Sea, this English rock band has a classic five-piece line-up with two lead guitar players (although this is the 2020s so they also play samplers and keyboards). The line-up is lead vocalist Conor Mason, guitarist Joe Langridge-Brown, guitarist and keyboardist Dominic Craik, bassist Philip Blake, and drummer James Price. In 2014, they signed to RCA Records and have now released four albums with the UK major. The most recent, *Dead Club City*, got to number one on the UK album charts. They made a switch to AWAL, a 'digital-first' label within the same umbrella of Sony Music Group. Smart move.

The band's debut album wasn't a critical success but has aged into something of a modern classic, containing a few genuine anthems. Singer Conor Mason has an unusual appeal combined with a signature voice with fantastic, operatic range, and the band is a growing force live (their 2024 Glastonbury set was impressive). They come across as a sort of modern incarnation of Led Zeppelin, and that's saying something. The fourth album is a watershed for good bands (it's the new "difficult second album") and *Dead Club City* paves the way for the band to go from very good to undeniably great. The band hasn't had any hits but doesn't need any – they have a sizable loyal fanbase that has grown through live shows and because their brand of 'pop rock' does well on streaming services. If anything, they are still underrated – a great place to be with the fifth album next up. In 2024 they embarked on a US tour – probably an attempt to break there. Whether it succeeds or not, the band has everything needed for longevity, including, most importantly, time.

Good luck to all of them.

APPENDIX – Five short case studies of longevity from the 70s to now

FROM THE 70S TO NOW: GARY NUMAN

Success came relatively quickly to Gary Numan, when his single "Are 'Friends' Electric?" (recorded with his then band Tubeway Army) rose to the top of the UK charts in May 1979. Without a chorus and clocking in at nearly five-and-a-half minutes, it was an unlikely hit record and the beginning of a rollercoaster music career. Its parent album, *Replicas*, released the month before, went to number one in the album charts, as did its successor, *The Pleasure Principle*, released a few months later. This album featured what is perhaps Numan's best known single, "Cars". He went out on a national tour to promote that LP, yet still found the time to write and record his next album, *Telekon*, released in September 1980, which also reached the top of the UK album chart. Three chart-topping albums and a national tour in less than 18 months is a remarkable achievement (matching The Beatles' first three album releases no less). Numan crowned off this period with three shows at Wembley Arena.

Perhaps not surprisingly, the 22-year-old was by then burned out, and he announced that these were the last dates he would play. He continued to release albums, though – and, in fact, returned to playing live quite quickly – but his career shifted into a slow downward spiral, despite high quality albums such as *Dance* and *I, Assassin*. Not only that, but Numan encountered another obstacle, that of a hostile media. The constant mockery by the music press and Radio 1's steadfast refusal to play his singles (in an aggressive strategy to *'re-youthify'* the station) meant that by the late 80s, Numan had mislaid his artistic vision as he struggled to write the kind of songs he thought people wanted to hear. He summed up his career at that stage: "I was nowhere. I'd lost my record deal. I was massively in debt. And no obvious signs that I would ever be able to recover that. My career looked to be pretty much finished."

In the early 90s, though, encouraged by his wife, Gemma, and inspired by Depeche Mode's *Songs of Faith and Devotion*, Numan decided to write the kind of album that *he* wanted to hear. The result was *Sacrifice*, an equivocal return to form, a trend he sustained on subsequent albums *Exile* and *Pure*. Once again, Numan's star began to rise, but this time as an artist seen as a notable influence and inspiration to other artists. In 1997 the release of a double album of Numan covers called *Random*, featured artists such as Damon Albarn, The Orb and Republica paying tribute to Numan's songs. Around the same time, rock band Nine Inch Nails were including Numan covers in their live sets. Suddenly, long scorned by the British music media, Numan underwent a critical revaluation. Over the last 15 years, he has released a further five albums, each achieving successively higher UK chart positions, with 2021's *Intruder* reaching number two. Throughout this time, Numan has continued to tour, with his concerts attended not only by the die-hard 'Numanoids' from his early successes but also a whole new generation of fans. Forty-one years after his farewell concerts, in 2022 Numan returned to the stage at Wembley Arena for a sold-out show as part of his highly successful *Intruder* tour.

FROM THE 80S TO NOW: JAMES

Manchester band James creates songs from jams. That's how they work. Nobody controls the process. Instead, their creative method is the band's four core members (Singer

Tim Booth, multi-instrumentalist Saul Davies, keys player Mark Hunter and bassist and founder Jim Glennie) jamming until the songs emerge. That's perhaps why uber-producer and electronic music guru Brian Eno put in a request to be the band's muse and produce their 1992 masterpiece *Laid*. James is driven to experiment, and it's remarkable that such fully formed songs as "Beautiful Beaches", "Sometimes", "Say Something", "Just Like Fred Astaire" or "Sit Down" all came from improvisations. Then again, the band will jam over 100 pieces of music and zone in on the best 10-15 to make an album, setting the quality bar high.

Tim Booth is one of those British lead singers that have slow-burned their way to becoming a national treasure. As Booth progresses through his sixth decade, he is the polymath one might expect - teaching transcendental dance, writing a novel, acting a little here and there and meditating throughout. Meanwhile, over the past four decades the band has survived members coming and going and the music industry changing beyond all recognition. The band owes its longevity to its unique penchant for risk-taking as a unit. After a long struggle to be recognised, James had a solid first decade, with distinctive hits and moderate UK chart success, but they have continued to release well-received music into the new millennium, with a late career resurgence.

As a live band, they are a force of nature, led by Booth's sometimes seemingly possessed performances. To see James in full flow can be a transcendental experience, but it's mostly a lot of fun and a sense of community amongst the band's audiences. Chart positions for the James albums have been a series of ebbs and flows, with a resurgence towards their 2024 album *Yummy* reaching number one in the UK chart. They have overcome several significant low points. Their 2001 album *Pleased to Meet You* was a critical and commercial flop, which led the band to break up for a period. Even so, from that album, their last single to chart was "Getting Away With it". That relatively unsuccessful single slow-burned its way to becoming the band's self-appointed theme tune and their third-biggest song on streaming platforms.

James has released nine albums in the current century but hasn't had a hit song since 1999. While Tim Booth is frustrated that his band are shut out of many routes to new audiences by radio and streaming editors, he also knows that this means putting more energy into new James music projects:

> There's something about listening to music when you're in your teens and 20s that you bond with that music in a way that you can't ever again. And so we can't have that impact with the new music we're making, because we don't have access to those young people. But eventually people will hear this music we're making now and they'll work out that it was as good as anything we made in the 90s. That's why we're selling out tours, which is more than we ever did in the 90s. We play all the new songs live, because it puts the pressure on us to make them as good as the hits. And that's a terrifying thing to have to try and do with a [new] song. But it makes us work really hard and it's a great way of forcing yourself into a corner.

FROM THE 90S TO NOW: NADA SURF

Stumbling upon a new Nada Surf record every 4-5 years is a highly recommended balm for modern-day life. Over the years, Matthew Caws' subject matter for Nada Surf's songs span life's day-to-day tribulations, the mangled thought processes that cycle through our brains, attention deficit disorder, and how to see light through a tunnel of bad news. As Caws himself puts it:

> There are some good things in life, one of those is the escape and the pleasure and the comfort of repetitive pop songs, and the hypnotic effect of chord progressions. There's a deal you make in pop music where you, as a listener, pretend this [music] is all new. Then a song will try and show you a good time.

Nada Surf songs are like the gift that keeps on giving if you look at a song that way. Alas, not a hit single amongst them. Nada Surf is one of those bands that made their way through a 30-year career and 10 studio albums without remotely disturbing the charts. Yet the band has never made a bad record and indeed Caws, modest to a fault, is somewhat coerced into being proud of never making a dud album: "It has felt great in terms of longevity for a very long time. Unbelievably when we were making *The Proximity Effect* (the sophomore album in 1998) most of the bands that we toured with had broken up and we were sticking together. That felt unusual."

In terms of being discovered beyond their core fan base, Nada Surf have found themselves featured on various shows over the years, including the massively popular coming-of-age drama *The O.C.* That helps. One of the key themes for longevity is the belief that your best work is always ahead of you. As such, Nada Surf struck gold once more with their 2024 album *Moon Mirror*. Their 10th full-length studio record was critically acclaimed and multi-award nominated, but, most importantly, gave the band a new lease of life. As they toured the record, the new songs went down well with their fans - as well as anything from their much-loved catalogue. Sometimes longevity comes down to keeping on, staying open to creative possibilities and not expecting too much, but the rewards become self-evident.

FROM THE 2000S TO NOW: MAXIMO PARK

Music critics have tried in vain to classify the music of Newcastle's Maxïmo Park, eventually converging on the term 'art pop'. Yet Paul Smith, the band's singer and main co-songwriter (with guitarist Duncan Lloyd) describes their music thus:

> Odd but still pop. Weird but anthemic. Music with a literary influence but also immediate – in some ways primitive – music that tries to slap you in the face a little bit, but twangs its way back to being pop. We try to make it accessible, if only to ourselves.

Only Paul Smith could describe Maxïmo Park that way. He wrote the marketing copy for the band's early gigs ('unruly pop' was one elevator pitch). With his art school background and literary leanings, Smith is very much the thinking person's pop lyricist. After early success (with their UK chart hits coming in a short burst, three from second album *Our Earthly Pleasures*), the band's ambition was to make every record different. With their third record, *Quicken the Heart*, different meant punkier, and the band's success stalled somewhat. For the next album, *The National Health,* the band brought back super-producer Gil Norton (who had supervised those early hits) to help get their mojo back. Despite not being a big chart success, *The National Health* saw Maxïmo Park get back on track, and they have steadily moved forward since, with higher chart placings and decent reviews. But the band has kept to its manifesto of celebrating its Northeast England roots. Paul Smith: "Bands should celebrate where they are from and not be ashamed of it. And if the music's good enough, there's a chance to create a legend."

It's a strong idea. A hometown is where an early fanbase converges and legend starts – a sense of place. Maxïmo Park has made its way to nine original studio albums. As 2025 rolled around, so too did their first significant anniversary – that of their platinum-selling, Mercury-nominated debut album *A Certain Trigger* (produced by Paul Epworth). Maxïmo Park celebrated with a reissue of the record and a UK tour performing it in full, a classic move that keeps their bandwagon rolling.

FROM THE 2010S TO NOW: VALERIE JUNE

Valerie June's path to cult stardom hasn't been easy. From the beginning, she sensed her journey would not follow conventional industry routes. While cleaning houses and working service jobs in Memphis, she received a clear vision that her music would instead reach people through her fellow musicians. As she puts it, "I had a vision that I would not make it – my music wouldn't reach its audience through regular means – it would reach its audience through musicians. My friends would help me. I'm a musician's musician." That early intuition shaped a career built through relationships, mutual recognition, and trust rather than music industry marketing.

Working through a talented community of musicians – one that has included Booker T. Jones, Brandi Carlile, Norah Jones and none other than Mavis Staples – eventually brought Valerie June an audience of her own. Her debut album, *Pushin' Against a Stone*, garnered rave reviews and entered the lower reaches of the UK and US album charts. Her subsequent four studio albums all met with critical acclaim, but June was never to become a chart musician. Nor does she fret over it. Instead, her standing with other musicians (Bob Dylan and Robert Plant are fans) and her joyous live shows are what provide the affirmation that her music hits the mark. She cites figures like Michael Hurley (a legend of American folk whose influence is deep rather than loud) as proof that a life in music can matter profoundly without mainstream recognition. "It's not about fame so much", she says. "That longevity thing is what it's about". As such, June is very much the modern version of a classic singer-songwriter – the kind of talent that would have been a household name on the music scene any time before the turn of the century. Alas, in the crowded space of the streaming age, she finds herself firmly in the space of a cult artist. And there's nothing wrong with that.

June has a signature voice – a reedy, twangy instrument all by itself – although she augments it with some pretty mean guitar playing. When combined with her spiritually influenced, post-genre songs, the overwhelming impression is that of an artist creating music out of time but classic, *timeless*. And she is also a poet, author and meditation teacher. It was Mavis Staples who opened her mind to the idea of making music with positive messages, something she has leaned into on all her albums, but most prominently on her fifth record, *Owls, Omens and Oracles*.

It's a cliche of sorts, but the power of artists in today's difficult times might be to entertain, but also to inspire, comfort, *awaken* – and help us learn to appreciate each other through the universal language of music. If you believe this to be true, then spending time with Valerie June's music might just change your life.

Acknowledgements

Thanks to all the bands and solo artists mentioned throughout the book, and especially to those who have joined me on *The Art of Longevity* podcast.

Special thanks to Brett Anderson of Suede, for inspiring this whole 'school project' (his words), and to Olly Knights of Turin Brakes, for being my first guest on a podcast that didn't exist until he was.

Thank you, Mick Clarke, whose illustrations for *The Art of Longevity* (and the cover pictures included in the Appendix case studies here) are always a delight.

Thanks to Fenner Pearson, for interviews and initial written work on both OMD and Gary Numan. And to David Freer for his interview with Stuart Braithwaite of Mogwai.

Thanks to both my wife, Angela, and to Emmanuel Legrand, for suggesting this book a long time ago. Thank you, Michael Muldoon, for copy edits on the very first draft.

Thanks to the team at Repeater/Watkins Media: Carl Neville (for commissioning and editing), Chris DeVeau (editing), Jake Regan (proofreading) and Christiana Spens (marketing).

All artist images included with the kind permission of the artists.

Gary Numan portrait original photograph by Chris Corner .

James portrait original photograph by Roger Sargent.

Maximo Park portrait combines a still from the video Child Of The Flatlands (directed by Greg Hodgson) and a separate portrait photograph of Paul Smith.

Nada Surf portrait original photograph by Jess Lomas.

Valerie June portrait original photograph by Travys Owen.

About the Author

Keith Jopling is a music strategist, podcaster and mentor. In 2021 he started the music podcast *The Art of Longevity*, and before that, the music curation, artwork and writing site *The Song Sommelier*. Keith has worked with the boardrooms of labels, streaming services, start-ups and investors. He has previously held executive roles with Sony Music, Spotify, EMI and the BPI. He began his career in music as Research Director at global trade body IFPI (2000-2006). As an educator, he has lectured in music business, strategy and innovation at Henley Business School, NYU, BIMM, ACM, Belmont, Syracuse, Westminster and the University of Krems, Austria.

Riding The Rollercoaster is his second book. He is also the author of *Body of Work: how the album outplayed the algorithm and survived playlist culture* (also with Repeater Books).

Also available from Repeater

Justify My Love: Sex, Subversion, & Music Video

Ryann Donnelly

In *Justify My Love*, Ryann Donnelly explores sex and gender in one of the most widely consumed art forms of our age — the music video.

Through an autobiographical reckoning with the author's life in a band and collaboration with past lovers, and a close analysis of the erotic iconography of music videos, *Justify My Love* tells the subversive history of this medium, from the inception of MTV in 1981 through to the 2010s.

Covering everything from Lady Gaga and Beyonce to Nine Inch Nails and George Michael, *Justify My Love* shows how subversion became mainstream, and how marginalised voices shaped some of the biggest music videos of the last thirty years.

Order online from RepeaterBooks.com

Also available from Repeater

Mixing Pop and Politics: A Marxist History of Popular Music

Toby Manning

Mixing Pop and Politics is not a history of political music, but a political history of popular music. Spanning the early 50s to the present, it shows how, from doo-wop to hip-hop, punk to crunk and grunge to grime, music has both reflected and resisted the political events of its era.

The book explores the connections between popular music and political ideology, whether that's the liberation of rock'n'roll or the containment of girl groups, the refusal of glam or the resignation of soft rock, the solidarity of disco or the individualism of 80s pop.

At a time when reactionary forces are waging political war in the realm of culture, and we're being told to keep politics out of music, *Mixing Pop and Politics* is a timely, original and joyful exploration of popular music's role in our society.

Order online from RepeaterBooks.com

REPEATER BOOKS

is dedicated to the creation of a new reality. The landscape of twenty-first-century arts and letters is faded and inert, riven by fashionable cynicism, egotistical self-reference and a nostalgia for the recent past. Repeater intends to add its voice to those movements that wish to enter history and assert control over its currents, gathering together scattered and isolated voices with those who have already called for an escape from Capitalist Realism. Our desire is to publish in every sphere and genre, combining vigorous dissent and a pragmatic willingness to succeed where messianic abstraction and quiescent co-option have stalled: abstention is not an option: we are alive and we don't agree.